The Distance Between Us

By
Bryon Hughes

Contents

Chapter 1

The sun reflected brightly off the windscreen of the nondescript white van, parked in the random space at The Trafford Centre in Manchester. Outside the van, mums with daughters argued about whether they would visit Selfridges or Debenhams first, and whether the Louise Vuitton or the Donna Karan bag would suit their sparkly dinner outfit best. Dads and lads discussed the day's game and who was tipped to score first. Laughing and joking, they all headed towards the entrances, eager to make the most of the first day of the Spring sales and bag a bargain or two, ready for the Summer.

Inside the van, Abrafo looked with disdain whilst he mentally checked his kit. Stun grenades: left breast, high explosive grenades: right breast, French made P90 sub machine gun: stripped and oiled the night before, ready in his hands. Extra grenades and clips in a shoulder bag ready to use, just as soon as he could get out to these vermin that he saw through the windshield.

These Khalets have bled our people dry for too long! Stolen our resources, killed our brothers, sisters, mothers and fathers and then branded my brothers the enemy!... all for this... Blatant greed and excess, whilst our people suffer! Today the infidel dogs will pay and I will be the hand of Allah in retribution! Abrafo thought. A fierce sneer scratched across his face.

Next to him, The two brothers Aziz and Amir, were also deep in thought. These brothers were legend in their homeland and came from an illustrious family of freedom fighters. Aziz, the leader of the group stood 6'2". He was tall for a man of his native Lebanon. His weathered tawny skin had seen many hours in combat and the scars proved his presence. This was his unit. A born leader with a horrific history of terrorism, he carried a global bounty of over $2m, for his successes against the oppressive western states. Schooled in the art of subversion and guerrilla tactics through the mid eighties by the Palestinian Liberation Organisation in Beirut, he quickly proved himself, justifying his role as a key operative, for both Hamas and Al Qaeda, through the nineties and into the millennium. His ability to evade capture or assassination had led to his men calling him "The Mongoose." A brave an aggressive predator that thrived in the desert preying on vipers. He liked the moniker. Aziz thought all the western states were snakes.

Next to him sat his younger brother, Amir. He was Aziz' only sibling and his closest compadré. It was a rare occasion that these two were ever separated. Siblings, soldiers and best friends, together they believed they were invincible.

Amir's career was almost as illustrious as Aziz'. Once again trained by the P. L.O. and then trained by his brother, he was also in the top ten most wanted terrorists by the USA. He was skilled in explosives, advanced driving in most vehicles and a fully trained pilot. He was just as essential to this small group of freedom fighters, as his brother Aziz. As a team, they had proven themselves to be an unstoppable force for their parent group, "The Light of Mohammed". A shadowy organisation that had been successful many times, in striking a blow against western culture and their corporations.

Aziz looked at his Unit with pride and loyalty in his eyes. Tikrit and Mustapha were relatively new to the group, yet they had proven themselves to be valuable assets. Abrafo had been with Aziz from the beginning. Like his brother, Abrafo was indispensable to Aziz. They were almost symbiotic from an operational perspective. He would die for them all and he knew they felt the same way. They were closer than blood. Their bond had been forged in battle, united against a common enemy, in Allah's name.

Aziz checked his watch. It was time.

He had chosen this shopping centre as a legitimate target, for many reasons. It was the largest and most revered mall in Manchester. Security was negligible for such an illustrious altar to western decadence and it was close to the motorway, which led to the airport. This would mean a quick getaway with the Imam. If all went well, Aziz expected to be on a plane with his brother and the Imam within a couple of hours, heading to Oman and hopefully soon after, some "R&R". He had been operational for over two years and badly needed some down time. Aziz trusted his instincts and he also relied on his meticulous planning abilities. Attributes of his own character that he thought were gifts from Allah. Through the power of his belief in his god and himself, he was completely self assured, that what was about to happen was righteous and a guaranteed success. There were no nerves as he addressed the unit.

" Brothers, it is time…"

He put a hand on each of the shoulders of the two soldiers opposite.

"Allah is great and in his divine wisdom, he has chosen you; Tikrit and Mustapha to be his shining angels, today. I vow to honour our arrangement and ensure your families will want for nothing. Your sacrifice today, will be remembered for all time and the Shā-îr will sing of your courage, forever! I cannot thank you enough and rest assured, Heaven holds a special place at Allah's side for you both. Allah Hu Akbar!"

"Allah Hu Akbar!" Came the reply.

"Gentlemen, today we strike a blow in the name of freedom and continue our efforts to disrupt and destroy all that is oppressive in our world. Allah, as always, is with us and we should not fear death. We will prevail! Stick to the plan and we will be victorious, once again. Move out."

On a mission from his god to turn a day of selling and buying, into a nightmare of bleeding and dying, Aziz flung open the rear doors of the van and 5 masked figures spilled out into the afternoon sunshine.

Chapter 2

First through the door was Abrafo. He targeted a young girl with her mother and squeezed the trigger of the P90. A short sharp burst rang out and the daughter dropped. The mother started screaming but was silenced almost immediately by Aziz' own strafe. Blood started to swim across the floor. Now, there was panic.

A group of young men saw the blood and started yelling as they took flight towards the main entrance. Amir gave chase. Aziz looked left. It was fast approaching midday and already the main entrance was packed with shoppers. He threw a stun grenade into the crowd and shielded himself behind a pillar. The concussion blew a few people to the ground and there was mass confusion. Aziz stepped out and let loose with the semi automatic. Shoppers fell like scythed wheat, as he sprayed the crowd with bullets. The sound of sporadic gunfire was interspersed with the moans of the maimed and dying, in a sick rhythmical counterpoint.

A boy called forlornly for his mother, who lay dead at his feet. The pretty multi-coloured flowers of her dress, now soaked in her dark crimson blood. A young girl sat with her guts in her hands. A look of utter disbelief on her bloodied face. The colour and life slowly draining from her complexion, as her youthful lips turned blue.

Aziz felt the familiar rush of excitement, as he surveyed his work. Filled with a great sense of power, he wandered through the main doors and into the middle atrium. He chased a group of families further into a store, picking them off like targets in a video game. He didn't want to go too far inside the store, as the clock was ticking and he didn't want to close off his exit to any possible retaliators. He retreated the way he came in, spraying the shop floor with gunfire as he returned to his Unit.

Abrafo had been busy wreaking his own particular brand of mayhem in the main atrium. He moved slowly through the building, making sure to check every nook for a shivering, petrified mark. He loved to seek them out like a twisted game of hide and seek. He believed it was his duty to Allah to punish every infidel he could find. In particular, he took a perverted pleasure in seeking out the women. When he was dispatching these harlot western whores in the worst ways, he knew Allah was smiling down on him.

He walked past a garden divider in the centre of the atrium and found two men crouching in fear. How these western men are cowards!! Not once, on any mission has any of this weak, pathetic race challenged me! He thought as he ended them with the semi-automatic. Moving on, he saw a boy crouching behind a bin. These little devils are the very same, that grow up to pilot the planes and drones that rain death on our brothers!! He drew his combat knife and plunged it through the child's right eye.

He reached for the Glock at his side and murdered two men running for the escalator to his right. Behind and to his left, his squad were doing their best to cause havoc. Abrafo saw a petite blonde frozen in fear, in a clothes shop to his right. He quickly entered and was surprised by a male shop assistant, who ran at him from behind a clothes rack. At last! A man of substance! He thought. The boy lunged forward, holding a telescopic clothes hook but Abrafo side stepped the thrust and redirected the pole downwards. The boy lost his balance and realised his error, just as the combat knife plunged into his head in-between his jaw and his ear.

Abrafo turned his attention towards the young female, who by now was screaming relentlessly. She fell silent in sheer terror as he approached. The fear on her face, and the knowledge of what was next, made the blood rush in his pants. A sick grin spread across his face, as he pulled her backwards by her hair and spun her round to face him on her knees. He held his gun to her head.

"Please... I'll do whatever you ask, but please... Just don't kill me. I have a little boy at home. He needs his mother."

"Shut up, bitch!" Abrafo snarled.

He unzipped his pants and forced his member into her open mouth. The terrified girl turned away at first but he slapped her across the face with the side of his gun. This is all these western bitches are good for, he thought to himself. Looking up at the mirror in front of him, he saw the last of his squad pass behind them and so he pulled the trigger. The girl fell dead to the floor, with a scarlet fountain squirting from her temple.

Mustapha and Tikrit moved quickly through the main atrium as soon as the gunfire began. Their main objective was to herd as many of the shoppers as they could gather and get them into the food hall on the second level. The next part of the plan was to be executed there. They moved like a snake writhing through the chamber, gathering people from shops along the way and forcing them onto the escalators in the centre of the complex. A few shoppers tried to run, or duck into a hiding place along the way, but Tikrit was always there with his pistol. A few executions later and the shoppers lost all appetite to resist or run. Fear and immobility took hold of their minds, as the crowd filled the food hall with tears and cold sweat.

"Greetings everyone!! My name is Mustapha and you are all my guests for today. If you cooperate with us, I can guarantee your safety. If you do not cooperate, then you will suffer like your friends downstairs."

"We are a group who seeks the release of a Muslim cleric that has been unlawfully incarcerated by your infidel government. Abu Hassan is very precious to our cause and his release is not for negotiation. We require his release for YOUR release. This is a simple request that should be met easily within the day, then you may return home to your loved ones. Sit tight and all will go well." He lied.

"Now, I require all of the men to stand to the right, all of the women to stand to the left and the children to come to me.....NOW!!!"

There were moans of misery and tears from the children, as the two men viciously lashed out at anyone deemed to be too slow. Eventually the horde split into three groups. Tikrit gathered the men and trained them into a large outer circle facing away from the middle and ensured they all linked hands. The women were then arranged in a similar way a few meters behind them and finally the children were gathered in a tight group around Mustapha in the middle.

Tikrit ran around the food court and ensured all doors and entrances were locked from the inside, then placed claymore mines in a bid to booby trap any attempt at breaching them. All the while, Mustapha kept his P90 trained on the crowd. Outside, the sounds of mayhem rang out in a cacophony of noise as the brothers and Abrafo continued their onslaught. Somewhere an alarm sounded out continuously. Mustapha scanned the children. He picked out the prettiest girl of around 8 years old with pig tails and long blonde hair. A small spray of freckles splashed across her nose.

"What is your name, little girl?"

"Lauren." Came the response.

At the mention of her name, her mother cried out a whimper from the circle of wives, sisters and mothers.

"Leave her alone! I swear if you hu..."

"Silence!!" shouted Tikrit, as he slapped the mother hard across the face with the butt of his pistol. She stumbled, as her cheek began to swell and the girl started crying.

"I'm sorry, Lauren, but we have rules and one of them is DONT SPEAK UNLESS YOU ARE SPOKEN TO! IS EVERYONE CLEAR?"

Lauren looked up with defiance.

"How old are you Lauren?"

"Eight."

Mustapha thought briefly about his new bride who was also eight and a pang of sadness overcame him. A troublesome girl, he had exchanged her for five AK47 rifles and 500 rounds of ammunition, with the peasant farmer that worked the land outside the training compound in Tunisia. The girl was useless to her father and he needed the weapons for himself and his four sons, to stave off attacks to his flock from animals and the bandits that roamed the area. She was a good home maker now, because he had quelled her belligerence with a beating most days. She kept things clean and tidy after that. Mustapha knew he would never see her again. It was a melancholy thought that he pushed to the back of his mind. Instead, he wondered how good Lauren would be as a wife.

"Everyone turn around!" He shouted from the centre.

Everyone slowly turned to look at the little girl. Mustapha took out some tape and a sawn off shotgun from his duffle bag. He proceeded to tape the barrel to the little girl's neck and the grip to his own hand and wrist. He made sure that both connections were unbreakable.

"This little girls fate is in your hands. If ANYONE tries to run...attack us... or fails to shout out a warning if we are breached.. or in anyway hinders our operation, I will decapitate this beautiful, innocent little girl with this shotgun. HAVE I MADE MYSELF ABSOLUTELY CRYSTAL CLEAR? Good...You can all turn around now and thank you for your attention."

Tikrit gave a few a reminders as everyone went back into position. The scene was set. So now they wait.

Aziz, Abrafo and Amir continued their objective, to cleanse the area of any left over shoppers outside of the food hall. The mission was pretty straightforward; The light of Mohammed would hold the hostages until the cleric Abu Hassan was released to Manchester Airport. Aziz Abrafo and Amir would be escorted there with some hostages and then they would all leave together on a flight to Oman. Mustapha and Tikrit would remain behind and detonate two huge bombs which would kill the remaining hostages, once Aziz confirmed that it was ok to proceed. The Unit's secretive benefactor, who had financed all their previous missions, had been very clear about the last part. The hostages must die.

Amir was enjoying himself.

He always did when he was with his brother. No one believed in the mission as much as Aziz and he would do anything for his older brother, who had been his idol and mentor for so long. He was prepared to die for him today. As always, when he was with his brother, Amir felt absolutely no fear. All was well.

Just then, he saw movement on the upper balcony above them. The familiar shape of the black hat and the checkers were a dead give away. He was confused. Reconnaissance had proved that there was no armed security on site and certainly not SCO19. Armed response meant weapons and they had not been expecting that level of resistance, at this early stage in the plan!

The figure darted from one pillar to the next. Surely, they would not have time to respond so quickly!! Anger flushed his cheeks and he took aim. The figure poked their head out again and Amir wasted no time in burying a bullet into the hapless victim's head.

"Armed Response!" he shouted to his kinsmen.

"Suppressing fire!" Shouted Aziz as he leapt from cover and moved forward.

Instinctively, the three soldiers moved through the building covering each other with short bursts from the semi automatics. Armed response tried to return fire, but they we're no match for the fluid skill of the team. They retreated back towards a huge department store. Once inside they took stock. How did they get in here so quickly?! Thought Aziz. They should not be responding so fast! He felt something he had never felt before in his gut. Betrayal... But who is the traitor? He pondered.

"Get behind me, brothers. I fear we have been betrayed. I am pretty certain the Imam will not be released, no matter what we say. Mustapha and Tikrit can carry on their mission, however we need to retreat. We will continue to ask for the release of the Imam so as not to arouse suspicion but as soon as we can, we run."

"It will be better if we split up, Aziz. We each have a better chance of escape if we run separately." urged Abrafo.

"I will not leave my brother." Amir affirmed.

"Calm yourself, Amir, Abrafo is right we should split up, but you will come with me. We shall meet again at the scheduled place, my warrior," said Aziz, " and we will toast our victory and the memory of our brothers in arms."

"My Friends, until we meet again." Said Abrafo.

Then, after a brief but intense embrace between them all, Abrafo slipped into the store behind them.

Aziz scanned the area for any survivors of the first assault. He knew he would need a hostage to proceed with their escape. He also knew the police would be stalling him and if they didn't act soon, they would be facing more highly trained operatives from the SAS and British Secret Services. Suddenly, he heard a rustle from behind the coat rack to his left. Investigating, he discovered a young woman hiding in-between the rails.

"Help! ah! Help!!" She squealed, as Aziz grabbed her by her hair. He pulled her close to his body and put his pistol to her head.

"Be quiet, you stupid bitch!" he shouted, as he forced her forward out of the shop.

Amir fell in at close quarters behind his brother, facing the rear. He held his brothers bullet proof vest high with his left hand. He scanned the atrium with determination.

"Officers!! Officers hold your fire!! I have a hostage!"

He pinched the girl hard and she squealed. The insurgents immediately returned to cover so Aziz could continue with his demands, without exposing the brothers to possible snipers.

"I demand to speak with your superiors, NOW!" Shouted Aziz.

"Stand by!" A grainy voice replied from a mega phone, somewhere in the atrium.

In a Mobile Control Unit in the car park of the shopping centre, Chief Superintendent Lewis of the GMP knew he had little options. He had been given the tip off around 30 minutes ago and since then, the world had been a blur. The hostage negotiator was inbound, but wouldn't be at ground zero for another 10 minutes. Having done no specialist training in hostage situations, he needed time to think. A Constable approached and startled him off his train of thought.

"Sir, the insurgents have made contact in the main atrium and wish to talk with you directly. How should we proceed?"

Lewis knew he had to take control whilst he waited for his negotiator, so he ordered SCO19 to throw a radio and he opened a dialogue.

"This is Chief Superintendent Lewis of GMP. Who is this?" He growled.

"My name is irrelevant, it is only my wishes that you need to concentrate on. I represent The Light of Mohammed. I assume you have heard of us?" Aziz responded.

"Yes of course, your reputation precedes you." He gesticulated to one of the techs sat at the computer and mouthed the word "information" at him. He began typing.

"How can we help you, today?" He said sarcastically.

"We, the Light of Mohammed, demand the release of the Cleric Abu Hassan from HMP Wakefield, immediately. We demand his safe passage to Manchester Airport. We need a car to the airport for myself, my comrade and our hostage. We shall join the Imam on his flight and when our safety is affirmed from Muscat International Airport, my comrades in the food hall shall surrender themselves and release all the hostages into your care. Any attempt at breaching their position will end in annihilation. If our demands aren't met, it will end in annihilation. We will kill two hostages per hour until our demands are met."

" Look, you know as well as I do that in order to start the ball rolling, the Home Office will need to see something from you. They will want a hostage released in good faith, otherwise no deal." Gambled Lewis.

 Aziz expected this and contacted Mustapha on the encrypted short wave radio.

"Release two children from the food court and tell them to run to the South entrance."

Mustapha followed the order.

"You and you. You are brother and sister, yes?...You are free to go. Run for your life! Now! before I change my mind!!"

The two children just stood there, whimpering.

"What about my Mum and Dad?" asked the little boy.

"Run along, Son, I'll be right behind you." shouted a man from the back.

The boy and his sister didn't move. They seemed unsure.

"Go on now, kids!" Encouraged their father, in desperation.

The boy had one last look but couldn't see his mum or dad. With tears in his eyes, he took his little sisters hand and they ran for the exit. Aziz saw them run past and head for the South entrance. Around 20 yards from the door, a gloved hand grabbed the boys arm and pulled him and his sister to safety.

Lewis was given the good news and he breathed a sigh of relief. The little victories always count. He was pleased that two children had been released. It showed that the group were willing to negotiate and an absolute disaster could hopefully be averted.

A crackle came over the Arab's shortwave radio as Aziz contacted Mustapha.

"Stage one is complete. Maintain radio silence and stick to the plan. You are in charge at the food court now. Allah Ma'ak."

"SIR!"

Mustapha nodded at Tikrit. Both men reached into their Bergen backpacks and each pulled out a large package.

Chapter 3

Abrafo found his way to the staff area of the store and quickly moved to the cloakroom. He was looking for a disguise to help him escape. There was a young man cowering behind the door. He was physically shaking when Abrafo grabbed him by his neck.

"Where are the staff uniforms." He growled. His breath smelled like death, the worker noticed.

I-I-In th-that cupboard." he said, pointing at what looked like a closet.

Abrafo snapped his neck with a twist and marched to the door. Two girls who were cowering inside, screamed as he opened the door.

"Silence!" he shouted and the girls slid to the floor, whimpering with their hands raised in fear, shielding their faces. He turned his attention to the clothes hanging on the wall. He searched for something that would fit his smaller stature. Born in the Congo, he stood a mere 5'4" tall. He always thought it was due to the pygmy ancestry within his family. His face was thin and pointy, giving him the look of a weasel when he sneered. He had seen his family decimated in 3 separate wars in his homeland and blamed it on the western corporate interests in the area. The Congo's huge reserves of valuable resources had been the prize of many colonial invaders, however, he particularly hated the British firms and their interest in the diamonds of the region. He wanted to mount an attack directly against them, but he hadn't been able to convince his superiors that there was any benefit to the cause.

At the age of ten, he had witnessed his mother's torture, rape and execution at the hands of the local militia. They had tried to get her to volunteer the names of fellow protesters at a diamond exploratory mine, bought by a British firm in 1990. She had been picketing, along with many others, striking for a living wage, better working conditions and civil rights for the diamond workers. The militia had arrived in force and taken her and some others to a fortified compound. Many more had escaped the round up, so they tortured her for information about her collaborators. Abrafo was seized off the street and dragged to his mother. Being a devout Muslim, she was horrified that her son was made to witness such terror, but she still didn't capitulate. Abrafo saw this as his greatest lesson from his mother. Even facing certain death, she had stayed true to what she believed was right. This lesson is what fuelled his cold determination and fearlessness in combat. Driven by a deranged belief that he was on a righteous crusade from Allah himself, he had never felt remorse. They killed her in front of him soon after, leaving him alive to feel the guilt and shame of an impotent boy, unable to save his mother from the monsters at her throat.

Glancing at the diamond ring on one of the girl's wedding fingers, his anger exploded again. These fucking western dogs are so asleep to the suffering that is inflicted because of their lust for diamonds!! He raged, as he kicked the girl with the ring hard in the head and punched the other in the temple. They whimpered beneath him, as he turned his attention back to the clothing.

He found a standard shirt and pants with the store's logo emblazoned on it and dumped his webbing, rucksack and combat fatigues in a locker. He kept his knife and two stun grenades about his person, in preparation for his escape. He turned sharply and left at speed, through the loading bay at the rear of the store. He quickly got into character before rolling the shutter doors. As they crept open, he looked out with protracted fear on his face, eyes furtively darting left to right. These fools will take the bait, he thought. Far in front of him, just outside the kill zone, a wall of police cars and vans awaited. A police officer waved him out and he scurried like a frightened animal across the car park to where the fool stood.

"My God! My God! Thank goodness you arrived!" feigned Abrafo," I think they're killing people in there!"

"OK sir, you are safe now. I will need you to follow me." Abrafo quickly fell in behind the police officer," It's protocol to debrief you on what you know, Sir. Any information you can share with us will be most helpful, you see? What's your name?"

"My name is Peter Ali." lied Abrafo," I am a cashier."

"Very good, Sir. If you would kindly step this way, we can get you debriefed with the others."

Abrafo was led away from the kill zone around the back of the police vehicles. He was being led towards what looked like a makeshift processing area for some of the shocked and traumatised shoppers, that had somehow managed to escape the mayhem inside.

"Please Sir, I need to go to the toilet." Abrafo said in urgency. He had little time to make his escape.

"There will be time after your debriefing, Sir. Please follow me."

" But I REALLY need to go, Officer! I'll use the trees." Abrafo squirmed.

"Ah! Right you are, Sir.. Er, what about over there? I'll escort you."

The officer pointed toward a tree-lined embankment bordering the M60 motorway.

"Perfect." said Abrafo.

They moved purposefully between the parked cars and vans until they slipped behind a large cargo van. Seeing an opportunity that was out of sight, Abrafo turned on the Constable and plunged his combat knife deep into his throat. There was a look of great surprise on the man's face, as he desperately tried to claw at Abrafo. The Arab twisted the knife back and forth, making a gurgling sound in the officer's throat. A quick flick and a violent spurt of blood, and it was all over. Abrafo deftly rolled the body under the van and headed for the trees.

CSI Lewis was pacing back and forth in the MCU. He had winged his way through the first interaction with these bastards, but he could really do with some help.

"WHERE THE FUCK IS MY NEGOTIATOR??" He shouted at no one in particular.

Just then, a tall dark man of Arabian origin, walked into the Mobile Control Unit. He had a calm demeanour and an aura of authority about him, that suggested experience in these matters.

"Hello. CSI Lewis, I presume? My name is Abdul Omar and I have been assigned as your negotiator. Brief me on the situation, please."

"Well Mr. Omar, we have an unknown amount of terrorists holding captive an unknown number of people. Two children have been released and they have said that the majority are being held in the food hall. A further captive is being held by two terrorists, who are demanding a car to the airport and a flight out of the country with the Cleric Abu Hassan. All the hostages will be released on confirmation of their safe arrival in Oman."

"I see.... Do we have any names?" asked Mr. Omar.

"Not yet."

"OK. Our prime objective is the food hall. However, we will deal with the separate insurgents first. Patch me through to the splinter group and have a car ready for them at the South Entrance..."

Omar was handed a two way radio. He paced a little, biting his thumb whilst thinking. After a short while, he began.

"Hello, this is Mr. Omar. I am authorised to negotiate on behalf of his majesty's government. How can I help to resolve this situation?"

"I will assume you have already spoken to the officer in charge." Said Aziz.

"Indeed." Omar confirmed.

"We demand the release of our Imam Abu Hassan. We will be escorting the hostage to Manchester Airport where we shall board the same flight as Abu Hassan. All hostages will be released when we are free to leave the plane, in Oman. We will not hesitate to kill two hostages an hour until our demands are met."

Omar knew perfectly well that the British government do not negotiate with terrorists. Protocol must be followed however, so he sent the demands up the chain of command. The safe play at the moment, was to grant the car to the airport, split the group and neutralise them at the airport and the food hall separately.

"OK. We are just waiting for confirmation from the Home Office that the Imam is en-route to the airport. This may take some time."

"You have 30 mins." Barked Aziz.

Sir George Rathbone, the current home secretary, hung up the phone, sat in his chair and sighed. This was a crucial time in the whole process. Soon, all of the careful planning would come to fruition and the Sovereign Territories Defence Act would be real.

Things hadn't gone quite to plan, however. He had hoped all the terrorists would die together in the mall, but they had obviously smelled a rat! No matter, they will be taken care of at the airport. There's no way they could be seen to leave the country without being challenged, as it would give a green light for future terrorists to make similar demands. We don't negotiate with terrorists. It's as simple as that...or that's the spin that will be released to the usual media outlets.

In reality, the plan was to create enough fear and carnage, that the general public would have no choice but to unanimously endorse the new Act. The small print of which, would ensure him and his colleagues would make an absolute fortune. He laughed. It was so easy! These poor chumps who are doing the dirty work for us, actually believe they are furthering their own cause, too! He burst into a guffaw at the thought of it.

In Manchester, CSI Lewis was biting his nails.

"It's a negative from the Home Office, Sir." said a Constable.

"They want a breach. SAS are inbound ETA 15 minutes. They want you to stall."

Lewis and Omar expected this. The government never negotiates with terrorists, but he thought he might have another chance to pull a few more hostages out, before it all went to shit. The CTSFO's from SCO19 had already got eyes in the room and they could see hostages arranged in concentric circles. At the centre, one of the insurgents had a young girl with a shotgun strapped to her neck and a breach of the doors would trigger Claymore mines. This could get messy, thought Omar. He used the shortwave radio to contact Aziz.

"Hello Sir, we have secured the release of Abu Hassan and he is now en route to Manchester Airport. He has told me to tell you the phrase "In Babylon, the moon shines a crescent". You are now free to join him at the airport, via the vehicle at the South exit."

Aziz was shocked. He had contacted the Imam through his relative just weeks before and this was the exact phrase he needed to hear, to let him know that all was well. It was now apparent that Hassan had been compromised.

"Excellent news, Mr. Omar. As a show of good faith, we will release two more hostages."

Aziz needed to keep up the ruse in order to make their escape, so he contacted Mustapha and two more hostages were released. After they were safely with the GMP, Aziz started towards the South exit. Amir covered his back whilst the hostage squirmed in front of Aziz, fearing the gun at her head. They passed the armed police without incident and headed outside to the waiting car. The engine had been left running and there was a full tank. Amir and the hostage got in the front seats and Aziz slid in behind the hostage on the back seat. Amir put the car into first gear and they headed towards the car park exit. Immediately, a small convoy of police vehicles surrounded them. Two motorcycle outriders sped to the front and an armed response unit fell in behind them. A collection of other police vehicles also followed at a distance. Aziz looked on, intently. They were trying to close the jaws of the trap. Above them, the unmistakable sound of the police helicopter's blades could be heard over the car's engine.

"Amir my beautiful brother, we shall celebrate with Abrafo at the safe house tonight, but first we must escape. I have faith in you and Allah above, my Brother. Allah will guide you to safety!"

"Yes Brother! Your genius shines out in the darkness again! Haha! we will be heroes on our return!"

Aziz gripped his brother's shoulder, lovingly. He glanced skywards with a prayer to Allah, as the convoy sped away.

They moved swiftly from the Shopping Centre and headed anti clockwise onto the M60. They proceeded at high speed onto the M56 and headed towards Manchester Airport. Aziz released the safety catch on his semi automatic and covertly reloaded, as he prepared himself for the coming battle. The hostage, shaking with fear, prayed to her god as hot tears leaked from her tightly closed eyes.

"Brother. Say when."

Amir checked all his mirrors and saw his opportunity.

"Now."

Aziz immediately turned his weapon on the outriders. Two short bursts through the side windows and the battle began. The first outrider took a bullet to the elbow and two bullets to the head. The last shell, ricocheted through the side of his temple and exploded his left eye socket. The motor bike veered uncontrollably as he was blown to the side, pulling on the handlebars as he did so. The bike dug in and flipped, spinning wildly behind the brothers, as they accelerated quickly into the fast lane. The second outrider, in a bid to avoid the car, smashed into the central reservation, as Amir slid the car wildly to his left.

The cavalcade of official vehicles dropped the ruse, just as the first police bike smashed into the bonnet of a large police minibus following behind. It span off to the left, as the armed response unit took it's place in the pursuit. Two more outriders joined the chase from behind, as Aziz reached into his bag and pulled out two high explosive grenades. He pulled the pin on both, as his hostage screamed in abject terror. He leaned out of the back of the car and threw the first grenade in the direction of the armed response vehicle closing in on them at the rear. He counted down before dropping the grenade but his timing was off and it triggered harmlessly in the road.

Much of the civilian traffic behind them, had rapidly slowed to a stop following the explosions, so Aziz had a good view of the job at hand. Amir was busy up front, dodging in and out of the traffic, as Aziz adjusted his timing and released the second grenade. It was a direct hit and exploded right underneath the oncoming armed response car. There was instant carnage. The car exploded, taking one of the outriders with it and creating mayhem behind. Vehicles ploughed into the wreckage and a massive pile up ensued. The final outrider escaped any mishap, slowing down and pulling into the hard shoulder. Aziz wondered if he hadn't the stomach for death or whether he had been warned off by his superiors. Only one cruiser remained in pursuit.

"One left, Brother!" He shouted from the rear.

"I'm on it." Said Amir, as they raced on into the traffic.

Chapter 4

James Mackenzie was pissed off. Once again, he had no idea why she was in such a bad mood this morning. It seemed to be happening more and more, lately. There always seemed to be something wrong. Whether he forgot to put a wash on or... he had left the newspaper on the table or... he hadn't brought the milk in from the car! There was always some reason for her to put the boot in!

He sighed. Well, I'm not playing along tonight, I'm fucking knackered and I've had a shit day at work, he thought. If she wants to drag it out, let her. Last time I asked her 'what's up?' she said 'nothing' in that sullen tone that meant, 'if you don't know, I'M not going to tell you', so when I said 'OK that's fine,' she flipped! He shook his head at the thought.

"Fuck it. Not playing tonight." He said out loud, as he squeezed the steering wheel tight and then released.

Today had been a complete waste of time. He'd booked an appointment with a chain of motor dealers in Manchester. He was hoping to sell some of his company's motor cleaning products to the valeting bay, but after pitching to the MD, he was told they were under contract with that shit house Davey Dempsey. Dempsey worked for his closest competitor and with their cheap products and underhand bribes to the workshop staff, they had almost succeeded in putting James out of business in the area. He had kept a smile on his face and suggested they call when the contract expires. Twat! He slammed his hands on the steering wheel. I fucking hate that Davey with his shit multi-coloured suits and his ridiculous ties. He remembered an old skit on the TV about the definitive office twat called Colin Hunt and that made him laugh. Ah well... There's always tomorrow, he thought.

The news on the hour drifted into his consciousness as he glanced at the dashboard.

"....taking you straight to Trafford Park, here's our home affairs correspondent, Julie Ann Gardner, with a live report... So Julie Ann, what's the situation?"

"Thanks, Zara. Well I can tell you that at approximately midday today, an Islamic fundamentalist group, who call themselves "The Light of Mohammed", stormed into Trafford Park shopping centre and secured hostages in the food court. Initial reports say there are a number of casualties but it's too early to confirm numbers."

For Fuck's sake! These fucking idiots killing innocent people in the name of their god. Don't they understand the irony? James shook his head. 3000 gods worshipped on earth but only yours is the real one, hey? Fucking bawbags!

"...Yes Zara, the group have issued only one demand. The release of the radical cleric Abu Hassan from HMP Wakefield."

Yeah, right! As if that's going to happen! These idiots have got their heads in the fucking clouds! James thought to himself. He had always believed that the only purpose of religion, was to keep us fighting amongst ourselves, whilst the people in power take all the spoils.

"I'll have to cut you off there Julie Ann, as we are getting reports from the eye in the sky at ITN, that a police chase involving some of the terrorists on the...."

That's enough of that, thought James and he changed over to Smooth FM. He shook his head. In 50 years of fighting "fundamentalist terrorism", the UK and USA had done exactly nothing to prevent the deaths of many of their citizens, both at home and abroad, at the hands of terrorists. James had started to think this wasn't just a catastrophic failure by the security services, but it was a carefully orchestrated secret plan, to keep the general public scared and hating a common enemy, whilst both of the governments continued the global sale of arms and munitions. Perpetual war is BIG business, he thought.

Stevie Wonder was singing "Signed Sealed Delivered" and James smiled again. This was the song that was playing in the pub on his first date with Alice. She was so beautiful, he nearly dropped his pint of lager. He was entranced by her long jet black hair, which contrasted so well with her golden complexion and beautiful jade green eyes. She smiled and it was all over. He had never loved a girl so much and never been more infuriated by one, either! For 20 years they'd laughed, shouted and cried. They'd shared the birth of their son and the mourning of loved ones lost, and as much as she wound him up, he would always love her and their boy. His mood brightened with these thoughts and he hoped that she was in good spirits by the time he arrived home. Providing there was no traffic issues on the '56, he reckoned he should be home in 20 minutes. He was looking forward to cuddles in bed, when he swerved to miss a broken bottle in the road and it all turned to shit.

Chapter 5

Alice wondered where the fuck Jimmy had gotten to. He said he'd be home over an hour ago. Seething, she reached for her phone. Hitting the speed dial, she crossed her arms over her chest and waited. Straight to the answer phone. She gritted her teeth. Fuck it! we'll start without him.

"Andrew! Dinners ready!"

Andrew was busy in the other room. On that fucking machine again. He never gets off it, she thought. Alice was worried that he was becoming anti social because of his obsession with computer games. He didn't seem to mix well at school and he only had a few real friends. With Jimmy on the road all the time and Alice having her own job, it was hard to keep Andy occupied. She sighed. She felt like a failure at being a mum and it seemed Jimmy was never there to help out. Just like now!

"Andrew! Dinner! NOW!"

"OK MUM! GOD!! I just wanted to finish this level!"

Andrew stomped into the dining room and slumped in his usual chair. At the age of 15, life was pretty rubbish for Andy. Too old to be hanging around the park and too young to be able to go to the pubs and clubs, where he was sure all the best looking girls hung out.

There was a knock at the back door and Tony, their next door neighbour, didn't wait for a response before walking straight in. Alice was silently fuming. Just because he works with Jimmy, he thinks he is his best mate! Where he has gotten that idea from is anyone's guess, she thought. They hardly speak at work, because Tony works in the office, and Jimmy is always on the road. I really wish he wouldn't just walk in like that, thought Alice. He never uses the front door. Probably because he knows, he can't just walk in that way. There's nowhere to hide when he comes round the back! It pisses me right off! She thought. Cheeky bastard.

"Hey guys! How are we today? I noticed Jimmy's car's not on the front again. Is he late?"

"Oh err, hi Tony. Yes that's right, he's been stuck in traffic apparently." Alice fibbed.

"Ah well... I'll er catch him later, then. You're looking mighty fine today, Alice! He's a lucky man our Jimmy, hey?"

Alice cringed.

"Err yeah, thanks Tony... But listen, we are just about to sit down for dinner now, so can you come back later, hey? I'm sure Jimmy will be back in an hour or so... Oh and er... could you use the front door in future? This one will be locked." She smiled with her mouth but not with her eyes.

" Oh... Err ... Right you are, Alice. I'll see you later, then. Bye for now, Andy."

"Yeah, see you later, Tony." Andrew smirked, as Tony backed out and shut the door.

"Mum, he fancies you." Goaded Andy.

"Shut up, Andrew!" She said, as she flicked on the TV and the news blurted into the dining room.

"...You join us, as we report live from Trafford Park, here on ITN."

Back at Trafford Park, CSI Lewis was watching the body cameras of the Counter Terrorism teams on their way to their positions, when suddenly, from inside the food hall, there was the sound of prolonged shooting from the terrorists. Lewis was taken aback at first, but then his professionalism kicked in.

"All teams BREACH! I REPEAT BREACH! BREACH!"
There was no way he was waiting to find out what the fuck just happened. This whole operation was quickly going to the wall and he needed to rescue as many hostages as he could, before it was an absolute disaster.

On the roof of the food hall, the SAS team blew a number of holes through the glass panels that formed the roof dome and began to rappel into the vast space below. Mustapha and Tikrit, who had their instructions to end the siege one hour after they had spoken to Aziz, whispered a quiet prayer to Allah and detonated their bombs.

The combined explosion was massive and blew out the remaining glass in the roof. A huge fireball engulfed the food court. Skin and blood ripped through the air and was instantly cauterized by the intense heat. Organic mush, body parts, bones, blood and the eviscerated carcasses of people that had existed just moments before, were scattered and seared across the destroyed hall and out through the roof. Alarms sounded and huge fires raged, as hundreds of families lives were ruined, by the most devastating terrorist attack on British shores since the "War on Terror" began.

Two hundred and thirty seven men, women and children from places as far as Inverness and Exeter were killed in the blast. Fifty six were killed in the initial attack, not forgetting the two insurgents and twenty one members of the police and armed forces. These figures added up to a total of three hundred and sixteen men, women and children killed on a day out at the shops.

 The ripples of that terrible moment would be felt for years to come by the surviving members of the families.

Andy Thompson, a young father who got separated from his wife and their two children in the attack, never fully recovered from the murder of his family. Three years on and suffering from Post Traumatic Stress Disorder, he would be found swinging in the garage from a short noose. Racked with guilt, he wrote a suicide note telling of his joy at being reunited with his wife and family, and a curse upon Islam and all who follow that religion. John Jeffers, from county Durham, lost his wife and mother in the blast. He drank himself to death just two years later in a puddle of his own piss on the streets of Newcastle upon Tyne. Becky and Richard Brown, the two young children released from the food hall first, never got over the guilt of surviving their parents murder. Painful relationships and addiction followed, shattering two young lives into pieces, for reasons beyond their understanding. A common tale that's told the world over, when ordinary people suffer at the hands of tyrants and psychopaths.

Sir George clapped his hands and belly laughed, as he watched these lives destroyed live on his television screen.

This was perfect! Exactly how he wanted it to unfold! Two of his rag heads had escaped, but that was no issue. He was sure MI6 will have it all in hand, very soon. Time for public mourning and private celebration!

"Anderson! Prepare a press release..." Rathbone barked into his intercom and soon after, Anderson, Private Secretary to Sir George, shuffled in with a pad and pen.

"The Home Office is devastated to hear of this terrible atrocity on British soil. Our sovereign government sees this as nothing short of an act of war and will respond accordingly. We will NEVER negotiate with terrorists and they will never destroy the Great British tradition of freedom and democracy for all. Our thoughts and prayers are with the families of the deceased."

"I have that, Sir. For immediate release?"

"Of course. Let's run an emergency edition of Question Time tonight, promoting The Sovereign Territories Defence Act. Get the usual team players in. If we strike now whilst the iron is hot, the general public will be overwhelmingly supportive in its implementation. This heinous attack only goes to prove how much we need the extra protection this Act can bring!"

"Yes, Sir. Of course, Sir."

Anderson left.

The Sovereign Territories Defence Act was the perfect vehicle to progress his political party's agenda. Increased surveillance, custody without trial, more public money for defence contracts including MI5, MI6, the Armed Forces and the militarisation of the Police. Having a very nasty enemy that everyone could get behind fearing and hating, was a very useful political tool. When people are scared, they rally behind a champion. That champion was the STD Act. Of course, it was an added bonus that himself, and most of the cabinet, sat on the board of the Corporations engaged in the business of Defence. All of the Party's donors were making money and life could not be better. He sat back in his chair, contemplating a prosperous future with a smug look on his face.

Chapter 6

Amir was in 'The Zone'. All of his concentration was centred on driving. He was topping out at one hundred and twenty four miles per hour in the Ford Mondeo he had been given by the police, and he cursed himself for not demanding a faster police cruiser. He was approaching a lot of congestion and the traffic was starting to get thick on the road. He weaved in and out like a natural, in spite of the fact that the car was right hand drive. Aziz was reloading on the back seat of the car and doing his best to throw off the last remaining cruiser in pursuit. The hostage was pinned in her seat. Every muscle was taught in her body and her eyes were still streaming, as she continued to pray to her god. The cruiser behind was gaining on them.

"Put your foot down, Amir!! These Bastards are relentless!"

"WE ARE AT TOP SPEED, BROTHER! THIS PIECE OF SHIT WONT GO ANY FASTER!" Screamed Amir.

Aziz loosed a volley that peppered the hood of the pursuing car. At last the traffic dispersed for a while and Amir took flight in the middle lane. Accelerating hard and only a couple of feet behind, the cruiser was trying to tip the Mondeo into a spin. Just as Amir was passing a car to his right, it suddenly veered left, as if trying to avoid something in the road. Amir had no chance to correct his trajectory and all three cars smashed together in a deafening crunch of grinding metal and shattered glass. A small family car in the outside lane was also caught up in the collision. Amir's Mondeo slammed into the rear right side of the family car, sending it into a roll as it lurched sideways. The hostage was thrown forwards through the windscreen, as Aziz came over the drivers seat and smashed his face into the back of Amir's head. The car veered off the road and down the embankment to the left, as the police cruiser went into its own side spin, rupturing the fuel tank on the debris. The car and the unconscious occupants came to a halt about 50 feet away from the Mondeo, right next to the family car. From inside a little girl was screaming…

Alice was still fuming with Jimmy, but she was determined to try and have a normal family meal with Andrew.

"So, what have you done to today, Andrew? Anything exciting?" Alice said, with a slightly forced smile. Trying to get any conversation out of him was hard at the best of times, but he seemed to be glued to the Television, AGAIN! She knew she shouldn't have turned it on at the dinner table.

".... Andrew, are you listening to me?"

"Ssh! mum! look at this! it's live now on the M56! Terrorists or something!"

Andy was excited. Subconscious memories were being triggered, as he associated the scenes with his favourite computer game; a first person shooter based on a crack special forces unit. Alice looked at the TV. The reporter was narrating the scene from the helicopter.

"... with the hostage, travelling at break neck OH!! OH NO! There has been a collision!!" Andrew and Alice gasped. "... There looked to be a casualty thrown from the terrorist's vehicle. Let's pray it's not the hostage... Four cars have collided on the M56, due west of Helsby... Just looking back... Yes it seems the traffic has been slowed by police around 500 meters back so no issues concerning a further pile up... There seems to be some movement in the farthest vehicle but still nothing from the police cruiser on its back in the road, or the terrorists car, which has careered down the embankment...."

Resting against the central reservation, inverted in his car, James McKenzie regained consciousness and couldn't understand why he wasn't in bed. The whole journey home had seemed like it was yesterday, yet here he was, upside down and strapped into his seat. It dawned on him with growing alarm that he had been in a wreck. He mentally checked his body. He had a great pain in his shoulder, and a quick glance showed him he'd been cut by the breaking glass. Otherwise, apart from a dead leg, he seemed to be in control of his faculties. He unclipped his seat belt and crawled through the jagged broken hole left by the smashed windscreen. All the while, a small trail of fuel flowed from the damaged police cruiser following the ruts in the road towards Chester.

Further back, Amir was livid with anger. His head was pounding from the impact of Aziz' face. He turned to his brother to see if he was OK but he was unresponsive. Amir checked his brother's pulse and realised he was still alive. Praise be to Allah! He thought, as he unbuckled his belt and climbed from the window.

"Hey!.. Hey are you OK, Pal?? That was some smash there!"

Amir turned to see a short, stocky man with mousy brown hair and wearing a torn grey suit walking towards him. This must be the idiot that veered into me! concluded Amir and he saw red.

In full view of the TV camera on the media helicopter, along with an assortment of smart phones from the roadside and finally the police helicopter camera, Amir marched over to James and smashed him full in the face with his fist.

James was not expecting a fight in spite of his previous training as a boxer and staggered as the blow landed. Amir aimed a swift knee to the head, but Jimmy recovered quickly. He'd been a great boxer as a boy and a punch to the face was nothing to the tough Scotsman. Jimmy blocked the knee with his left arm and swung hard from below with his right fist. Amir just simply wasn't ready and didn't see it coming. Jimmy's fist connected hard with Amir's chin in a crunching uppercut, that shattered an incisor and knocked Amir out cold. Aziz had since come round and climbed the bank to witness the assault. Enraged by what he saw, he raised his pistol and fired twice.

All around the country, in pubs and homes, social clubs and at work, millions of Britons witnessed the spectacle on live television. Including in the dining room at Jimmy's house.

"Jesus, Mum! They just shot that man!!"

"Language, Andrew!..." retorted Alice, "Oh my god! I hope he's alright..."

Two bullets ripped into Jimmy. The first catching his thigh and the second hitting him in the left shoulder. He was thrown backwards by the force and hit his head on the ground. Instantly, the white searing pain simultaneously exploding from his thigh and shoulder, prevented him from passing out but he felt very groggy as Aziz ran over. Ignoring Jimmy, he lent over Amir. He was still out cold.

"Amir! AMIR!!" He slapped him hard, but no response.

Jimmy thought it prudent to lie as still as he could be, even though the pain was like nothing he'd experienced before.

Aziz had a tough decision to make.

He tried to lift his brother but to no avail. He had to think! If he tried to take Amir with him, it would mean they would both be easily captured. Think... THINK!... Aziz growled forlornly as he realised he must leave his brother to the enemy. Fear and a deep sense of foreboding smeared across his face, as he understood exactly what that meant.

He needed transport and quickly. The eastbound side of the motorway was moving past slowly and he could see the idiots in their cars holding their smart phones up to him. He scanned the traffic and saw a motorbike weaving in and out of the lanes. In one deft move, he vaulted the central reservation and shot the rider as he had almost pulled alongside. Grabbing the motorbike, he turned it around and headed down the hard shoulder to the nearest junction. The police chopper followed him.

Back at the roadside, Jimmy was in terrible pain but he managed to get to his feet. Blood was pouring from his wounds and he was feeling more and more light headed. He smelled petrol fumes really badly and looked down to see the trail of fuel. Muffled cries for help came from the police cruiser, so he shuffled over.

Two officers were trapped.

One was conscious but the other was out for the count. Jimmy kicked hard at the windscreen and yelped in pain as he took the weight on his injured leg. He picked up a rock from the roadside.

" Cover your face!" he shouted as he hurled the rock at the screen.

Again the pain was immense but he was successful.

"I.. I've injured my leg," said the driver.

"Join the club, pal!" Jimmy said as he fell to the floor and grabbed the officer.

Together and through great pain, they cleared the wreck. Jimmy went back for his partner. Just then, fifty metres down the road, the fuel stream pooled by a discarded cigarette butt. For a moment, it looked like the pool would flood the butt and simply extinguish the cigarette. However, just enough time passed for the fumes to accumulate and ignite it, before the butt was submerged. Fire raced along the trail back towards the car and set it on fire.

Jimmy knew he had little time.

Summoning up all the energy and willpower he had left, he shuffled back to the cruiser and wrestled with the belt on the unconscious man. The heat from the flames was melting the paint on the car and hurting his face. Come on... Come on!! His hands just didn't seem to respond under the pressure. Finally he released the belt. With all his might and with a huge cry of pain, he muscled the young constable free from the car.

Just that little car now, thought James. He staggered over to the car while panic started to take a hold. The cruiser had been burning for a minute now and he feared an explosion. Inside, a young girl was conscious whilst her mother, who was in a terrible way, was incoherent. Jimmy grabbed her first and got her to a safe distance, then went back for the child. She was screaming and in tears.

"Hello darling, let's get you to your mum, hey?"

Jimmy was covered in blood and must have looked terrifying. He unbuckled the belt easily and beckoned her out. No Time! no time! Thought Jimmy, as he picked her up with his good arm. He got ten metres from the car when there was a massive explosion as both of the cars lit up the late afternoon sky. Shrapnel peppered Jimmy's body and a large chunk of metal glanced his head, whilst he shielded the little girl from the white heat and intense flame that engulfed them both.

Everything went black for Jimmy, but the whole world watched live on Television, as the damsel was saved and a national hero was born.

Chapter 7

Nathan Cromwell dashed into the office more concerned with how he looked, than the unfolding national disaster happening before his eyes. With a superior air of authority, he breezed through the cramped cubicles on the journalist's floor and barked,

"Meeting in my office, NOW!"

A gaggle of reporters and hack "journalists" dropped everything and jumped to his order like prisoners of war.

"Jayne, what have we got!"

"OK so...at approximately 11.45am, a terrorist group known as The Light of Mohammed stormed The Trafford Centre in Manchester. They demanded the release of Abu Hassan, the radical Cleric, and transport for them all, in a bid to escape to the Middle East. Obviously, our government refused to deal with them and the subsequent breach by our special forces ended in tragedy. Two terrorists and two hundred and thirty seven civilians dead in the explosion, fifty six were killed in the shopping centre spree and twenty one serving members of the Armed Forces and Police." Jayne looked excited. "Also, we have a car chase ending in one terrorist escaping and another being captured, solely down to a have a go hero, who dropped him after a collision at the roadside. This guy's amazing, by the way! He gets shot and then goes on to rescue two police officers, a mother and her daughter before being blown up and air lifted to hospital! He's critical but fighting!!" Jayne couldn't contain her excitement.

"CHRIST IN HEAVEN! LADIES AND GENTLEMEN! THIS IS THE STORY OF OUR LIVES!!"

Nathan was shaking his fists wide eyed with glee.

" Jayne, as soon as we are done here, I want you to get over to the hospital and find out who he is, where he's from... what makes a hero like this? Is he a family man? Regular church goer? All the details! Dave, I want you to run with the main story. Break down of events, government response.... You know the drill. Roger! get on the sensational daily comment.... Something along the lines of "Liberalism allows terrorism. The STD Act is our only safety net..." come back to me with something snappy and concrete. Everyone else get to it! We've got a national disaster here and a bloody national hero! I want the story now!"

Everyone leaped to their feet. Mobile phones sprung into silicon life with a symphony of electronic bleeps and buzzes, as the daily hounds got on with the job selling fiction as fact. Nathan slammed the office door. Only Jayne was left.
Nathan placed his hand on Jayne's hip as she was attempting to leave the room.

"Jayne, can I have a minute?"

"Anything for you, handsome!" Jayne gushed.

"Just a word before you leave, darling. I couldn't say it in front of the others because eyebrows would be raised, but I want you to do whatever it takes to get in with this guy. Wear a shorter skirt, bat your eyelids blah blah! you know the drill. We NEED this exclusive darling and if you land it, the sky's the limit for you. I promise I will PERSONALLY take care of it! These fucking rag heads think they rule the world, Jayne! I was talking with Ben at church on Sunday and he says they are planning a fucking invasion through Europe via refugee camps! For Fucks sake! Good job we're here to expose them, hey?"

Jayne looked on with a mixture of admiration and naive love. She had come as an unpaid apprentice to the paper, just six months before. Nathan had made no attempt to hide the fact that she had got the job because of her "nice ass" and she loved it. Always the quiet girl at school, she was often picked on for her plain good looks, by the fat bitches who couldn't keep their feet out of the chip shop, never mind on the running track! Now this fine specimen of a man, with all the power at this paper, couldn't keep his hands of her. She revelled in the attention and wasn't even bothered about his other girlfriend at home. Anyway, she was on the payroll starting from this month and she had plans of stealing him away with a beautiful flat in Islington.

"Why thank you, kind sir! I'll do my sexy best as always." She turned around and stuck out her "nice ass" for him to admire.

"Are we going for dinner after work tonight, Nathan?"

She gave him that coy look, whilst twiddling her hair through her fingers. She thought it made her appear innocent and sexy.

"Mmm… not sure we are going to find time with this story, darling. I can't rest until I know we've got the exclusive on this hero!"

Jayne loved it when he was intense! He was so passionate about his work and it got her damp. She didn't give a shit about the story, she just wanted to climb onto his cock. She remembered how it tasted.

"Just before I go, pull the blinds, Nathan... I have something for you."

Chapter 8

Where the fuck IS James?! Alice was starting to lose her temper. She had tried his phone a few times now and it was ringing out at first. Now it was turned off. If he's with that bitch, I'll fucking murder the pair of them! Alice was positive that James was seeing that girl from work called Chloe. He was always impressed by one thing or another that she had gloriously achieved! Running for charity or, taking care of her disabled mother or, saving the fucking world with one beautiful wiggle of her young, blonde, tight, little....fringe! Alice fumed. Then, there was all that talk she heard from Tony, about that "incident" at the works party. She couldn't wait for the next one, so she could confront her and Jimmy about it together and see if they were lying!

"ANDREW!! Come and load this bloody dishwasher! I'm sick of asking you to do your chores! It's like groundhog day in this house!"

"Alright mum! I'm just on the toilet!" Andrew lied. He was texting Kate, again. She was fit! Andrew had admired her at school for years. She was often paired with him in class when teams were needed for a task and she always made him laugh. She had fiery auburn hair and green eyes that he couldn't stop staring at. Sometimes she would catch him doing it and smile. His plan was simple. Keep her laughing and then slip a kiss in at the end of term dance. His plan was working great, if only his mum would just get off his back!

"ANDREW!!!!..."

"ALRIGHT!!" He shouted and whispered, "for fuck's sake", under his breath.

The doorbell rang and the knocker sounded at the front door. That was strange, thought Alice. Most people just use the doorbell. She opened the door.

"listen, I'm not buying... Oh..."

"Hello….Mrs. Mackenzie?" Two uniformed officers stood in front of her, it was the female asking the question. What's Andrew been doing now! She thought to herself.

"ANDREW?!! GET HERE, NOW!"

"CHRIST MUM, CANT I HAVE A MINUTE TO..."

"Mrs. Mackenzie, can we come in please? We have some news about your husband..."

Alice was confused, made all the more unnerving by the ball growing in the pit of her stomach. Just then, Andrew joined them at the door.

"Oh er... You better come in then... "

Everyone filed into the front room, where Alice sat in her chair and the two officers sat looking uncomfortable on the couch. Andrew lingered by the door.

"Mrs. Mackenzie your husband has been in an accident on the M56 today. Have you been watching the news, at all?"

Alice was totally taken aback. She immediately felt ashamed and guilty. Her anger melted like a snowflake on a hot car bonnet.

My poor James!

"What happened? Where is he now?... I need to be with him."

"It's a little more complicated than that, I'm afraid. He was involved in the collision, following the terrorist attack in Manchester, on the M56 earlier today. I'm sorry to tell you Mrs. Mckenzie but James has been shot."

Alice felt like she had been punched in the stomach hard. Tears welled in her eyes.

"He is in a critical condition at The Countess of Chester hospital. He was evacuated by air ambulance and is currently undergoing surgery."

" Oh my god!" Alice whispered. Hot tears escaped her eyes and fell on her chest. She realised immediately that the man she saw getting shot on the television was Jimmy and she had an overwhelming urge to vomit. She struggled to keep her dinner down as she spoke.

"I must be with him. Come on Andrew, get in the car."

"We shall escort you Ma'am." Said the policeman.

"Thank you, Officer."

Tony watched from the window of his house, adjacent to the Mackenzie's as they left. He ran to the front door, accidently booting his pet terrier, as he fervently grasped the handle. It yelped and ran to the kitchen.

"Everything alright, Alice?" He shouted from the doorway.

"No Tony! James has been shot! He was caught up with those terrorists, today. I need to be with him!" She said as she continued to weep.

"Can you watch the house for us?"

"Christ Alice! Yeah er sure... Give him my best, will you?"

Tony walked back into the house. Well that's a turn up for the books! He thought. He fantasised a little about James dying and comforting Alice through it, but he quickly dismissed the idea.

"You're horrible sometimes, Tony." he laughed to himself.

Chapter 9

Aziz had been watching the safe house from over the road, for three hours. He had observed intently, as vehicles had come and gone in the street. He had surveilled for any suspicious looking vans or cars in all of the approaches and the roads surrounding the house. Experience had taught him to be patient and do his home work, before taking any major decision. Whether or not Abrafo had been compromised and the house was now a trap, was yet to be discovered. Aziz sighed. My gut tells me its ok, he thought. He always trusted his instincts.

Aziz inserted the key into the lock of the door and rapped "Asfar" in Morse code on the knocker. The Arabic name for yellow was chosen as the password, if they were to arrive separately. Abrafo lowered his semi automatic machine gun and embraced his friend as he came through the door.

"Brother!! You are alive! Praise Allah!... but where is Amir?"

"Abrafo... I...... I had to leave him at the roadside. He was unconscious and if I had tried to rescue him, we would both have been caught." Aziz spat violently on the floor. "Curse those fucking pig dogs!"

Abrafo was dumbfounded. "Aziz, I'm so sorry...." There was nothing to say that could console Aziz, so he just embraced him again.

Aziz was beside himself. Everything had gone wrong and he felt like it was his fault. My baby brother!! Inside he was teetering, but he could never show it to his men. His men! Ha! What was left of them!

"Abrafo, today was a great victory for The Light of Mohammed and everything is as it should be. Amir is in Allah's hands now and I know he will keep him safe. Habibi."

"Yes, Sir!" Abrafo stood to attention and saluted. He didn't know what else to do.

"At ease soldier, tell me of your escape."

The pair moved to the kitchen were Aziz opened two bottles of beer. Abrafo told Aziz of his disguise and how he escaped over the embankment. He had crossed under the motorway via a roundabout and had stolen a car from a dealership not far from Urmston. He had arrived around an hour before Aziz and had waited anxiously for his comrades.

"My brother, you have done well! I will see to it that you receive a bonus for your exploits today. Our benefactor will be pleased!"

"Thank you, Sir. So how did you escape?"

Aziz explained every detail up to the crash.

"I escaped on a motorcycle I stole from a rider. The Police Chopper was following me so closely, though! I rode around two miles further down the road, where I saw a motorway junction. Underneath the junction, on the roundabout, Allah had left me good fortune! A passer by had pulled in to talk on the phone. I immediately commandeered the vehicle and made my escape." Aziz laughed bitterly," The Chopper had no idea until it was too late."

"... and what of the passer by?"

"Dead in a ditch on the way here."

They both laughed whilst Aziz took out a bag of Cocaine. He separated two lines and offered a bank note to Abrafo.

"What to do next, my Brother." Pondered Abrafo.

"Our benefactor will contact us shortly with an exit plan, I'm sure." Asserted Aziz.

Abrafo took the note and snorted the Cocaine handing the note back.

"Yes, Sir."

They retired to the TV room to watch the drama unfold on the late news, drinking beer and snorting well into the early hours.

The next day, Aziz was already awake when Abrafo came downstairs at the safe house. He prepared a simple breakfast of flat bread and hummus and took it into the front room, were Aziz was on a secure phone call.

" Yes sir.... Absolutely...my heart grieves, Sir, but I know we must be strong. Sacrifices must be made.... Yes, Sir. We shall speak then..." Aziz terminated the phone call.

"So what's next, Brother?" asked Abrafo.

"We are to wait for further instructions. There is too much heat to consider leaving the country, as yet."

Secretly, Aziz was burning inside. Even when the heat has died down, how can I leave my brother here at the mercy of secret service agents, in the UK? How do I explain to our mother, that I abandoned Amir? He was always her favourite. His parents were no strangers to war and bloodshed. They fought for their native Lebanon, through the long civil war that enveloped the country after independence from the French was declared in 1946. Maybe she would understand and yet its never easy, when the casualties of war are your family.

Aziz had been fighting Christians all of his life. His father had been murdered by one when Aziz was a young boy and he had never fully understood why. Raised in a devout Muslim home, he had learned that his religion was borne from a thousand years of war with the invaders from the West. Crusade after Crusade to secure the Holy lands for Western states, had left his ancient kindred decimated, enslaved and robbed of their land and resources. Islam was born out of a resistance to this invasion. It brought order and discipline to the ancient tribes of Arabia and trained them into a formidable army to withstand the infidel hordes from the West. This new Islamic Army, galvanised under the one true God, Allah, expelled the infidels from the holy lands. Political and military expansion followed soon afterwards, creating an empire founded on stability and prosperity. Fast forward 2000 years or so and his kindred are STILL fighting the same war for resources and land against the Infidel invaders! A war that they were losing.

Sit back and do nothing? Welcome to oblivion.

Stand and fight? Branded a terrorist.

Aziz felt despair regularly, but he would fight on until the end to avenge every man, woman and child murdered in the name of the Christian God. He knew that his daily struggle was Allah's great trial for him. In this way he could prove his worth and enter the gates of heaven a worthy man. Some days, he thought Allah must be so disappointed in his efforts. Like today.

Chapter 10

Jayne Carraway walked with elegance and charm, through the reception area at the Countess of Chester hospital. She wore a low cut black dress by Chanel that finished way above the thigh. It shimmered due to the fine material that was perfectly stitched together to accentuate her feminine beauty. She wore four inch heels from Leboutin. Stunning in black, the thin straps had tiny Swarovski crystals that meandered all the way around her ankles, highlighting their delicate curvatures. Jayne had finished the look with some silver bracelets and a necklace from Tiffany. Always careful to play down the jewellery, as not to take the attention from her alluring, symmetrical face. Her hair was curled and blown to perfection and she had the smokey eye shadow, that every man she had ever encountered, just could not resist. All heads turned, man or woman, as she walked through the gaggle of journalists and TV crews. She felt invincible as she made her way to the elevator.

In spite of her youth and her "bimbo" good looks, Jayne was an intelligent, resourceful and persuasive manipulator. Jayne had called the hospital earlier pretending to be James' sister and successfully duped the receptionist into revealing which room James was making his recovery.

Alighting the elevator in a breeze of Chanel No 5 she feigned sadness and glassy eyes, as she approached the officers, standing guard outside of the room.

"Sorry Miss, no one but family are allowed in."

"But I am family, Officer! I'm James' sister Jilly and I've travelled a long way to see him."

"Do you have any identification, Miss?"

Jayne fumbled in her purse pretending to look.

"I think I've left my licence in the car... is this really necessary..."

Just then, Andrew emerged from the room and was immediately taken aback by Jayne's beauty. A typical 15 year old boy, his hormones were racing everyday and the mere sight of a beautiful woman, was enough for him to lose his common senses.

"Woah!" He exclaimed.

Jayne acted quickly.

"Ah nephew, there you are!" She took a chance. All or nothing.

"Nephew?!" Andrew asked as she gently but firmly dragged him down the corridor and out of earshot.

"Please don't make me out to be a fool to the Police." She said, turning on the charm. "You must be James' handsome son!"

Andrew was impressed that she thought he was handsome and pushed his chest out a little.

"My name is Jayne, what's yours?"

"Andrew. So why are you saying you're my Auntie?" He asked, laughing a little and trying to look cool.

"I work for the best newspaper in the world and we want to make your dad a hero! Would you like that?"

Andrew would have agreed to anything she said at this point and blurted out, "Yeah!"

"Well, I have a letter that I'd like you to pass on to you're parents. It's got my name and number on and if you could get them to call me, we can discuss how we can make your dad famous and rich!"

Andrews eyes widened and a big smile spread from ear to ear.

"RICH?! OK definitely!"

"You are such a special guy!" She said, whilst leaning in and giving him a kiss on the cheek. Andrew blushed.

"Make sure you get them to call me within the hour Andrew, otherwise I can't hold the front page for your dad, and that would be bad."

She coyly pulled a sad face and then smiled.

"Can't wait to meet your dad, and I especially cant wait to see you again, handsome." She said, whilst giving Andrew a cheeky little wink on the side.

With that, she turned on her heels and walked back to the elevator. Andrew watched her go and caught himself looking at her perfect backside, hypnotically moving with her hips left and right. His cheeks flushing red, he quickly looked down at the envelope and wondered if he should open it. He decided against it, as he would probably get a clip around the ear from his mum, for being nosey! I wonder how rich we are going to be? Andrew thought, with a huge smile on his face. He just needed his dad to wake up now and everything would go back to normal. Well as normal as it could be with a huge wedge of cash in the bank! He mused.

Andrew, grinning from ear to ear, nodded at the officers and returned to his family, full of hope for the future.

Chapter 11

Amir had woken to the sound of the Air Ambulance landing. He had already been hand cuffed and was then quickly huddled into the back of a waiting van. There was no markings on the side and that led him to believe it was a government vehicle, probably MI6. These assumptions seemed to be correct, as he now found himself bound to a chair by his forearms and his shins. He suspected strong leather or material straps but he couldn't be sure, as he had been hooded throughout his journey.

They had driven for some time at speed without turning, before slowing down to city speed limits with a number of turns. He had been counting quietly in his mind and by the estimated time, and with the pattern of the journey, he guessed he was somewhere in Manchester. He was aware of a light above his head... incandescent... A bulb of sorts, as opposed to a strip light. He could tell by the warm colour temperature showing at the base of the hood. It was cold and damp, suggesting he was underground or even in a shipping container or garage. He listened intently for other give away sounds but none where forthcoming yet. No one had come to him since his arrival. It was all part of the plan of action, he thought. He had studied the interrogation methods of his enemies. It was a double edged sword knowing what was to come. He was prepared but also scared. Very scared, but they would never know.

"AMIR ABDUL KHAN. WE KNOW EVERYTHING ABOUT YOU AND YOUR FAMILY. WE KNOW ALL ABOUT YOUR PAST CRIMES AGAINST THE INNOCENTS OF MANY NATIONS. YOU HAVE NOTHING TO BARGAIN WITH AND YET IT IS MY RESPONSIBILITY TO EMPTY YOUR HEAD OF ALL USEFUL INFORMATION BEFORE YOU ARE BROUGHT TO TRIAL FOR YOUR CRIMES."

"FUCK YOU!" Amir retorted. "You talk to me of 'crimes'?? How about the children of Gaza? How about our babies in Iraq, Afghanistan, Syria and Libya?? You fucking disgraceful bastards are so brainwashed, you think you're bringing 'freedom' and 'democracy' when all you bring is death, and yet you take EVERYTHING that is not nailed down! WHO IS THE REAL CRIMINAL HERE?? GO TO HELL!!"

Amir's mind was working over time. The voice was distorted... Disguised with a pitch shifter and a vocoder. There was no way he could identify the speaker from the sound of the voice .... He would have to try a few tactics to see which interrogator he was dealing with. Amir knew, that because of his high status as one of the most wanted men in the world, there would be a possibility of only three interrogators.

For some time now, The Light of Mohammed had a mole on the inside of the allied counter terrorist movement. This is how they had stayed one step ahead of their pursuers after each successful mission in the past. Aziz had always been privy to mission critical data that had been relayed to him from the top of their organisation. This suggested to Amir that someone with top security access to western intelligence was on their payroll. When this became apparent, their unit had asked for as much Intel as possible about their adversaries in the security services. Through the information provided, they had been given details on interrogators they would most likely face if captured, in a bid to prepare for their methods.

Even though he was taken in the UK, the most unlikely out of the three would be the British interrogator, Mathew Davidson. He was a middle eastern specialist for MI6, fluent in 8 languages including his native Lebanese. He was known for getting results without torture. The second choice would be the American Dan McCallan. A big bruiser of a man who's favourite techniques included sleep deprivation and water boarding. The last, most likely and by far the most frightening to Amir, was "The Israeli", Solomon Horowitz.

Born of a Polish Jew and a Nazi Officer of the Einsatzgruppen, his paternal father had raped his mother in the woods surrounding Kyiv in Ukraine, before boarding her on a train to Belsen, in the Autumn of 1942. There, she kept her bastard secret from the guards, by hiding him in the shit troughs during inspections. Amir wished he had drowned down there, for Solomon was an animal.

"AMIR, I DONT HAVE TO TELL YOU HOW MUCH TROUBLE YOU ARE IN, YET IT IS IMPORTANT FOR YOU TO UNDERSTAND, YOU ARE NO LONGER A CITIZEN OF ANY NATION AND THIS LOCATION IS NOT CLAIMED BY ANY GOVERNMENT. NOBODY KNOWS YOU ARE HERE AND NO ONE CARES. THIS IS A BLACK SITE, AMIR. DO YOU UNDERSTAND YOUR CURRENT PREDICAMENT?"

Standard interrogation techniques, thought Amir. Create a feeling of being isolated and work on the morale. Amir remained silent. He needed more time to try and work out who he was dealing with.

"YOU ARE ALL ALONE, AMIR. WE CAN DO WHATEVER IT TAKES TO GET THE INFORMATION WE REQUIRE. DO YOU UNDERSTAND?"

"FUCK YOU!" Amir screamed.

There was a short pause and then the doors flew open behind him. He heard them clang like a great bell tolling. Next came a blinding white flash behind his eyes, followed by severe pain to the back of his head. He barely had time to register what was happening, before his body was targeted by the assailants and he was racked with pain again. He could see nothing but it seemed like a hundred blows were upon him, concentrating on his chest, arms and legs. It seemed to last an eternity, but Amir never cried out. He needed to appear tough at first, then slowly seem to give in to their demands. It would make his cover story appear more truthful. Finally, with a brutal blow, a cascade of excruciating pain erupted in his left arm, as a telescopic truncheon smashed into his humorous bone. This time he couldn't hold in the scream.

"ALLAH DOES NOT SEE YOU WHEN YOU DO NOT REPENT YOUR SINS, AMIR. ALLAH HAS FORSAKEN YOU. YOUR COUNTRY AND YOUR BROTHER HAVE FORSAKEN YOU. YOU ARE A RUDDERLESS BOAT CAST OUT FROM SOCIETY, MY BOY. YOUR ONLY REDEMPTION LIES IN ABSOLVING YOUR TORMENTED SOUL TO THE ONE TRUE GOD, YAHWEH."

The weight of the words hit Amir's stomach like a cannonball. He broke into a cold sweat, as his left arm went numb and the tip of his little finger raged. Only The Israeli would use such religious words for he excused his savage ways, as many do, by a staunch belief that he was doing his god's work.

The irony of that statement was lost on Amir. Like so many before him, he would rather deny his own hypocrisy by lying to himself, than admit the blasphemous sins he had committed that went against his own God's doctrine. Still, he had prepared long and hard for this eventuality. He sighed, heavy with trepidation. He knew he must maintain his façade for now and give nothing away.

" I will tell you nothing!!" He spat.

"Oh but you will. All in good time, Amir. We would like you to settle into your new environment for a while. We have some surprises for you but they will take time to arrange. In the meantime, make yourself at home."

Horowitz had at least a few days, maybe a week or two at the most, before he would be fully equipped to interrogate Amir. He knew it was a pointless exercise before all the pieces were in place. 2 weeks was plenty of time to soften him up, though. Cracking such a brutal nut will take patience, he thought.

Chapter 12

James had been taken out of the induced coma yesterday and since then, he had been peacefully sleeping. He was dreaming about spiders right before he awoke. Alice had been given the good news and had spent the whole night awake by his side, expecting him to open his eyes, but as usual, James had kept everyone waiting! He came round to see his wife's face smiling down at him.

"Hello handsome, how are you feeling?"

Uh oh! Thought James.... What have I done now? She never smiles and calls me handsome! He became vaguely aware that this wasn't his room and a wider look, told him he was in a hospital bed. Andrew was sitting on a chair just behind Alice, looking the most attentive Jimmy had ever seen him, when he wasn't playing on his games console. In the background, there was the familiar bleeps and tannoy chatter that accompanied any visit to the hospital.

"Hello Petal, how ya doin?" James said in his broad Glaswegian accent.

Alice beamed and burst into tears. James memory started to come back in fits and starts. He remembered being late for dinner on the '56... Oh!... He remembered the bang, but nothing after that...

"So, I guess I'm lucky to be alive then, Hen?"

This set off another bout of tears from Alice and Andrew came over for a hug. James winced a little when Andrew squeezed him, but he didn't mention it. It was years since he'd cuddled his boy.

"Hey! what's all this guys? I'm fine, just now!" James laughed.

"Can you remember what happened, Dad?" asked Andrew.

"Not really, Son. I expect I had a crash, didn't I?"

Alice gripped James hand tighter than a vice.

"There's a little bit more to it than that Dad..."

Andrew stood and pressed play on the DVD player underneath the TV. In the few days that James had been in the induced coma, Andrew had gathered a few news reels, as a visual scrap book for his dad. It had the added benefit of giving him something to do, so he didn't feel so helpless whilst his dad lay there, unresponsive in bed.

The first scene was the news report from the helicopter, that showed a police chase as it raced down what looked like the M56, just after Runcorn. The police were weaving in and out of traffic quite dangerously and sporadic bursts of gun fire could be seen from the car being pursued. Bloody hell! Thought James how did I get mixed up in this? Just as he was thinking this, he witnessed his own collision from way on high and the experience was a little surreal. Instantly, he had memories rush back to him and a huge pang of pain emanated from his shoulder where he must have sustained a big injury, he reckoned. The reporter's voice sensationalised the scene in the background and James' mind was racing. He saw himself climb from his car and the subsequent fight. He saw himself get shot! The scene unfolded on the screen and James sat in astonished wonder, as the explosion enveloped him and his precious ward.

Andrew had edited the viewing soon after and the motorway was replaced by live scenes from The Trafford Centre. The reporter explained the situation in the background as James tried to comprehend what he was seeing. There was mayhem as people were leaving the building. The scene switched to a distant view from a camera on a roof top, looking at the dome on top of the food hall. Suddenly, there was a massive explosion and amongst the debris, James saw tiny arms, legs and torsos get blown into the grey Manchester sky.

"I'm going to be sick..." He mumbled.

James fought to hold his breakfast down as he considered everything in his mind. Of course he was disgusted by it, but he understood why it happened, probably more than most. This knowledge filled him with despair and sadness regularly, but never as much as it did right now.

Since the dawn of time, people had fought over land, resources and domain over people. It was nothing new to the world, but with the dawn of the industrial revolution, the business of war had taken a more sinister turn. He was aware of how the great families of the world had consolidated their power over the years. Back in Napoleonic times, the Rothschild family had financed both sides of the war between England and France, and had profited greatly from the arrangement. It was no surprise that wars were now manufactured to feed the insatiable demand by investors, for record profits from the Military Industrial Complex.

The United States of America had been at war for all but seven years of its existence. There must always be a bogeyman for the nation to rally against. Initially, it was the British, then each other, followed by Mexicans, Germans, then Communists in South East Asia and across the globe, and now Muslims in the middle east. This kept the fires at the armament manufacturers burning and kept the coffers of the share holders full. Political stooges in office had kept it all on the right side of the "law", whilst they lined their own pockets with vast sums of blood money. As long as it wasn't their kids dying in the mud, they would turn a blind eye. Of course, everywhere you kill innocent people, their family's turn to revenge and the great cycle continues. The never ending war on terror IS the terror and yet, the majority of people were still so blind to see it. It was infuriating.

"How many died, Son?"

"Hundreds dad, many of them kids..."

James closed his eyes and shook his head as tears escaped. "That car you collided with was the terrorists, Dad. You knocked one of them out! You're a national hero!"

"I don't feel like one right now, Son." James mumbled.

Next on the show reel was an interview for the local news. Apparently they had had a feature just based on him. He couldn't believe it, fame at last! He thought sardonically and let out a sarcastic chortle. He instantly regretted it, as the pain bloomed in his chest. Billy Mac from down The Lion was on the screen, with some of the pub lads in the background. The interviewer was asking a question.

" So tell us more about James...What's he like as a friend?"

Billy Mac laughed," He's a lovely fella with lots of friends here! Always helping everyone out if he can. He'll be nice to a fault, ya know! As for that Arab lad, Jimmy was never gonna take that lying down! Haha"

All the lads started laughing in the background and Andy let out a laugh, too. Jimmy shifted uneasily. He had never really sought the lime light and it didn't sit well with him, that he was on the news in these circumstances.

"Everybody loves you Dad, even the papers..." Andy was beaming. He handed his dad the latest copy of The Daily National, and on the front page was a picture of him smiling at a football meeting for Andy's Sunday League. It seemed one of the other parents from the team had decided to cash in quickly on their association with him. Grunting, he quickly returned his thoughts to the photograph. That was a great day! Come to think of it, it was the last time he remembered that Alice was truly happy. Andy was 10 years old, and he had only been playing with the team a year, but they had fought to win the league. That day was the day they were crowned Champions. They had had a picnic in the park afterwards and he remembered, he had never seen his wife look more beautiful, than when she laughed that day. A warm smile spread across his face.

The headline was "Mackenzie for G.C!" With a picture of the George Cross emblazoned on the right.

"What a load of bollocks!" James blurted out loud.

"No Dad, it's true! Everyone thinks you're a hero! You want to see the cards and flowers at the house, Dad! George at The Lion says people have put so many beers behind the bar for you, that you won't have to buy a drink for the next ten years!"

They both laughed loudly.

"How do you know that, Son?!" James asked.

"Tony told mum when he popped in yesterday."

James had a side ways glance at Alice, who looked everywhere but at James and his smile turned to a sneer.

"Oh really, Son? Tell him I said hello, will you? "

"OK, dad." Andy was still beaming as he started to read the article.

Alice hated the way Jimmy inferred that she liked the attention from Tony, especially when all the rumours were about him! Swiftly trying to change the subject, Alice took out the letter from Jayne. Andy had passed it to her after Jayne had left. It was very intriguing! The paper had offered them a lot of money for the rights to James' story. A LOT of money! Far more than any other reporter had promised.

"Darling, have a look at this." She handed him the letter. "Obviously you have a story to tell and it's open to the highest bidder, currently held by these..."

"Andy, do me a favour, Son. Go and get me a cup of tea from the café, will you?" said James and handed him a ten pound note from his wallet.

"OK, dad. Can I get a chocolate bar too? " He ventured.

"Go on then! Don't say I never give you anything!" joked James as his son left the room.

The smile left James' face abruptly as soon as the door closed.

"Tony been round again, Alice? What's the excuse this time? I'm fucking sick of him flirting round you and you doing nothing about it! He'd stop it if you said something! It's like you're doing it just to wind me up!" James was fuming.

"Don't fucking start, Jimmy! Here ya are, ill in bed with gunshot wounds and all you can think about is riding my arse over that shithouse next door? For fucks sake man get a grip!" she retorted, " Stop ya greetin and read that bastard letter, won't ya?" she snapped.

James read the letter.

"Jesus Christ!" he laughed, as a broad smile enveloped his face.

Chapter 13

Nathan Cromwell was watching the TV intently in his office at the papers headquarters in London. The dinner time news was giving an update on James McKenzie live from the hospital. Just the usual shit, thought Nathan. No one knows a fucking thing! The programme switched to a live broadcast from James' local, were pictures of him were hanging from the walls and tacky bunting littered the ceiling. The interviewer was talking to a punter.

"Does this kind of response from James surprise you?" they were talking about his now legendary punch that floored one of the rag heads.

"What from Jamsie? Haha not at all! Takes no lip our Jamsie, mate! Does he lads?"

There was a low playful grumble from the lads in the background. The country was obsessed with this man and Nathan badly wanted his story! This could mean a raise for him and maybe a promotion to the board. A different punter at the pub was giving his tuppence worth in the background, Christ! How he hated the scouse accent. Fucking thieves and low life's the lot of them!

"You know, I think our Jamsie deserves a medal for what he's done!"

More cheers erupted from the crowd. Nathan sneered, shaking his head. There was a knock on the door and Jayne danced into the room with some paperwork placing it on the desk. Maintaining eye contact, she coquettishly leaned over the desk in front of Nathan. He felt a pulse in his pants as he spanked her backside hard.

"What the fuck is going on with the scoop on McKenzie, Jayne?!" Nathan was playful but he was beginning to feel irate.

"There's not much else I can do, Nathan. I delivered the letter and left my number. His son seemed well taken with me, so I guess we just wait?" Jayne replied testily.

Nathan roughly grabbed her backside and lent into her ear.

"That's because you're an absolute diamond, darling!"

Jayne let out a nervous squeak and flushed a little in her cheeks. God, he was so sexy!

"I bet you one of those rats at The Chronicle has got in and offered them more! Fucking cunts..."

Nathan hated losing and especially to those fake stuck up bastards down the road.

"I want you to get over to the house and wait for the wife to arrive. Explain we will match any offer they've got and you have my permission to increase it by 100 grand. You got that, my little fuck puppet?"

Jayne blushed again. She loved it when he was so confident. She loved to be dominated. "Yes, Sir!" she shouted with a mock military salute and left the room.

Nathan was left alone in his office. For fuck's sake! A million not enough for these trogs?! People just take and take these days. Like the fucking rag heads, always wanting more. Piling on boats to flood Europe with cheap labour. Stealing everyone's fucking jobs and plotting our down fall. Fucking muslims make me sick! He thought, seething.

Nathan gathered his coat and left the office. It was time for Mass again. He had always been a devout Roman Catholic and believed in his God absolutely. His faith had been shaken a few times; when his mother had died of Cancer, when his marriage had failed, but none more so, than when his older brother, Harris, had been killed in the second Gulf War.

Harris had been in Baghdad in the final days of the war. He had been assassinated by an insurgent in the Green Zone, one week after the ceasefire had been declared. The Cunt who had fired the shots was an Iraqi policeman. He had used his position to get close to Harris' unit, killing four of them before he was taken out.

Less than a handful of Allied troops had died in the whole conflict and yet God had chosen to take his only brother. It was hard for him to reconcile his death, but the Priest at St. Joseph's, Father Doherty, was there to explain God's purpose when Nathan was at his most vulnerable. God always takes the best to fight his eternal war with Satan, and Nathan firmly believed that that was where Harris was right now. Fighting the demon fucking rag heads at the side of God and St Michael.

Nathan had sworn to publicise just how demonic these bastards are, by making journalism his life's work. His aggression and work ethic made him an absolute asset to the right wing media in the UK. Lately, a wave of fervent Patriotism had gripped the nation after the Muslim aggression of the last decade, and he had rode in on the wave. Nathan had excelled in patriotic articles that touched the Nationalistic nerve of the Great British public. He exposed the flaws in immigration that lead to Muslim families draining the benefits system, the criminal Muslim paedophile gangs in the north of England and he had unmasked the horrors of forced marriages and "honour" killings in Asian communities. All this crusading had ensured a swift promotion to Editor in Chief at the paper. His kind of Patriotism was just what the owners loved. The owners being best friends and business partners with his Father, had also helped his rise through the ranks, but Nathan played this part down a lot, when bragging about his career to anyone who would listen.

His phone buzzed and vibrated in his pocket.

"Jayne, my darling! Give me the good news...."

"Mr. Mackenzie has been in touch, Nathan! We didn't have to negotiate and he's prepared to give us a three part exclusive for his life story, commentary on the accident, his views on Islam and the UK's response. He's given us global rights in print and the internet! We've got the lot!" Jayne was almost hysterical.

"JAYNE YOU ABSOLUTE BEAUTY! Meet me after mass at the flat, it's time to celebrate!"

Fucking excellent news! Thought Nathan. The man is a national treasure already and we have him to ourselves. He clapped his hands and rubbed them with glee. The readers will lap this up, he thought, as he closed the lapels of his coat against the evening chill.

Chapter 14

In the days that followed the attack, Abrafo and Aziz had been very disciplined and adhered to protocol. They never left the safe house, as there was no need. All of the necessities of life had been provided by an old lady, Manal, that called once a week with full shopping bags for them. She had been recruited to help maintain the safe house and keep it well stocked. She was paid handsomely and was a loyal servant. Their favourite food was Tabikh which they found to be both delicious and excellent for keeping their spirits high, as it reminded them both of home. Other staples were Tahini, houmous, flat breads, lamb shoulder, goat pieces, chick peas, mint, parsley and rose water. Many spices were to be found in the pantry such as cinnamon, cumin, sumac, all spice and coriander. Aziz was insistent that Manal mix up the Lebanese groceries with a lot of standard English food. Although they never ate the horrible processed food that the English so readily accepted, he was paranoid a strict Lebanese diet would raise suspicion with the shop owners. Not all of his Arab neighbours were sympathetic to the cause and he didn't want any unnecessary attention being placed on Manal. He had little faith in her ability to withstand interrogation.

Abrafo was very easy going when it came to food. He would eat very little and not very often. Aziz was convinced this was more to do with his Cocaine habit than anything else. Manal would bring the cocaine with the shopping and Aziz wondered if he would have to start to ration Abrafo's habit. Aziz could take or leave the white powder but Abrafo seemed to need it a little too much. The daily boredom that always accompanies staying out of sight, obviously has something to do with it. They would try to break it up with weapons drills, computer games, keeping fit on the indoor gym and lots of prayer, but the truth was it took a lot of self determination to keep focused.

Aziz' mind constantly wandered to the attack and the subsequent capture of his brother. His glorious baby brother! What were they doing to him?! Where was he? All the unanswered questions started as a whisper but as the days rolled on they turned to a deafening shout in his mind. He struggled to maintain discipline and more and more, he began to blame himself. If only he could have carried Amir across the road and into another car, they may have escaped. If only...

The constant murmur of the twenty four hour news broadcasts was incessant in the background of daily life. Every channel reported on the new "National Hero" McKenzie. Aziz fucking hated that Khalet! If it wasn't for him and his fucking car, Amir would still be by his side! From the papers to the news channels, every reporter was idolising this man. Calling for him to be knighted and given medals! Simply for getting in the way! He was deeply worried about what was happening to his baby brother, but slowly he was replacing those thoughts with renewed hatred for this "McKenzie" man! He smashed his fists against the coffee table in front of the sofa where he was sitting and jumped to his feet. The stinking British loved this man so much.

Aziz fumed as he paced the front room of the bland Semi Detached in Walkden. Slowly an idea formed in his mind. Maybe thought Aziz, this could be worked to our advantage... Maybe we could seize Mckenzie and exchange him for Amir! There is no way that they would sacrifice such a publicly idolised man. The hated British government would have to give way on their policy of non negotiation with terrorists. The general public would be in outcry! Aziz smirked. This just might work…

Aziz dialed the number and waited.

"Hello. Yes I know you said not to contact you and await further instructions, but I am not happy leaving my brother to these dogs…"

Aziz spoke for a few minutes and then hung up. Once again he was told to await further instructions but no matter. He already knew he was going to rescue his brother, whether it was financed by his mysterious backers, or not. It was a matter of courtesy to let them know of his plans. That was all. Now, down to the nuts and bolts of it. How do we snatch this McKenzie man?

"Abrafo, we have a new mission."

Chapter 15

Solomun Horowitz awoke in the apartment overlooking the Mersey, in Manchester. He had dreamed of his sister again and had woken with a desire to see her. His work kept him far from home most of the time and he hadn't seen his sister since Passover, two years ago. Being in this line of work meant that the fewer ties you had, the less chance of being compromised in an unfavourable position. Solomon had no children and no sweetheart. It was for the best. He had never been one for children, or love for that matter. He didn't understand emotion, Although it did fascinate him.

The apartment was loaned to him by the British Government. He was there under extremely clandestine circumstances and so there would be no official paper trail and no record of his visit to Manchester. The apartment, like Solomon's mind, was meticulous and exact. The neutral greys and off white tones blended nicely with the surrounds of the river. The bathroom was clean and ordered and there was no food in the fridge or cupboards. Solomon travelled light and needed only two identical outfits. He wore fine Italian suits by Rubinacci with a blue silk tie, Italian loafers by Velasca and 2 beautiful Rubinacci white shirts, made from the finest cotton. Each day he would have his attaché dry clean the one he wore.

Solomon turned on the shower and observed the unbranded cleanser and shampoo. Anonymous, just like himself. He stepped in and began to wash. Yahweh had always provided for him and in return he did God's work. The eternal struggle between the chosen and the heathens had been his personal mission since leaving school.

He knew he wasn't like other people from an early age.

He struggled to maintain relationships in his youth and was more concerned with how he could manipulate people to his advantage. People were a great resource to him. After finishing his National Service with the Israel Defence Forces, he had re-enlisted as an Intelligence Officer. Having gained experience sharpening his skills in seeking out Hamas in the Gaza strip and the West Bank, he was quickly promoted. His emotional detachment and surprising mental resilience to inflicting torture on Government captives had become apparent to his superiors. They chose the path of interrogator for him and his career really took off. He never told his mother and sister of his work and they never asked. With over 20 years of service to God and his chosen people, Solomon had become legend in the darkest of professional circles. He was the bogeyman. He was the go to guy when there was no one to go to. All of the Western Allied Security Services were aware of his skills and he was a man in high demand. There was no limit to his methods or his brutality, which is why he was always so busy, and yet officially, he was never there.

He stepped out of the shower and dried himself in the mirror. Damn! I'm good looking! He thought. He flexed his muscles and turned to look at his ass. He was getting hard. Time for one tug before I roll, he thought. Today, I crack Amir Khan.

Chapter 16

Tony peered through his blinds as Alice, Jimmy and Andy pulled up outside his house. There was absolute mayhem in the Cul de Sac. The road was completely taken over by news vans and satellite dishes. Reporters and television crews descended on the family like hyenas, trying to pull them apart, this way and that, eager to secure some meager scraps of an interview, for the 6 o'clock news. Tony watched as Alice fought them off with that fiery attitude he was so drawn to. One day he would tame that fire for himself, he thought.

Even his own house had been under siege, as reporters had harangued Tony night and day, for an interview about his neighbour. He wasn't going to give his story up about Chloe that easily, though! He was waiting for the hero worship to get to fever pitch, before approaching the tabloids with his date rape bombshell! If he waited for the right moment, he would definitely maximise the value of his story, especially if he made it an exclusive. Give it time, he thought. The papers love to create and then destroy public heroes! It's how they keep the sales coming in, he assured himself.

Alice looked amazing in Tony's eyes, marching through the media throng. She was wearing a beautiful summer dress that he had never seen before, which had pretty red flowers on it.

Christ! He wanted her!

Jimmy was never around and he could tell that she wasn't happy. After he had fed the lie to her about that business with Chloe from Accounts, Tony had seemed to be the shoulder to cry on for Alice. He liked that a lot. She had confided in him, on a number of occasions, about what she thought was going on with Jimmy and that "Hussy". Still, he hadn't seen an opportunity to throw the lips on her yet. Never mind, he could always take the scenic route to her hot pocket.

"If nothing else, I'm a patient man!" He sniggered to himself.

He watched her closely as they walked into the house, peering at her backside most of the way. I'll give it thirty minutes he thought, and I'll steal round the back again. It's worth seeing what shit I can whip up between them, over this present from everyone at work. Maybe a juicy little argument might be worth something later on, for the big exposé!

"Ah! Home, sweet home!" Jimmy said as he took off his coat and threw it over the end of the bannister. "I've missed my own bed!" he exclaimed, with a big smile on his face.

Alice barely smiled back at him. All she could think about was how irritating it was that he kept doing that with his coat! For Christ's sake! She was sick of telling him to hang it up properly! She kept her mouth shut this time, though. She thought she would give him a break, as he was just getting home from the biggest ordeal of their lives.

"Put the kettle on, love!"

Yeah... back to being the normal skivvy in the house then, thought Alice as she stormed into the kitchen.

Andy disappeared almost immediately into his bedroom, with the familiar sound of his games console starting up. Jimmy slumped into his favourite chair by the fire and marvelled at how much he'd missed doing nothing and watching TV from his favourite spot.

Alice came in with a cup of Javan coffee. The special beans Jimmy liked from the supermarket, that smelled gross to Alice, but he loved them.

"Ahh thanks, Petal! My favourite biccies, too!" boomed Jimmy, as he wolfed down three Jaffa Cakes in as many seconds.

Alice caught herself judging the way he ate the biscuits and made a mental note to stop being so hard on him. It seemed everything he did lately was getting on her nerves and it was difficult to see past it. She left the room to put the laundry on.

Jimmy was still recovering from his injuries and he wasn't a young man any more. He hadn't been able to stay awake for too long since he began his recovery, and with the heat from the fire, he slipped off into a dreamless sleep. He wasn't sure how long he was out, before he heard the back door open and a familiar, annoying voice.

"Hey guys! I saw you come back and just wondered if you needed anything bringing in from the shops? Only too happy to help with anything, really!"

Jimmy grimaced. That annoying prick from next door, again. Jimmy was on to Tony from the start. He had seen how his eyes wandered to Alice, when he thought no one was looking. He knew he would try his weasel best, to get into her knickers if he had half the chance, and all this faux good neighbour stuff, was really starting to grate on Jimmy's nerves.

"Oh, Hi Tony, Jimmy is in the front room." Alice said, dismissively.

She waved him through from the kitchen, while she busied herself with the dirty clothes. Tony couldn't help a little naughty thought, as he walked past Alice on her knees.

"I'll go straight through, then," he said, staring at her chest as he passed.

"...and how's the big fella feeling?!" Tony shouted, as he bombastically jumped into the living room.

"Aye not bad, lad." Jimmy said, trying to look groggy so he would fuck off, quick.

"I'm so glad you're home and on the mend, mate. What a crazy situation that was, eh?"

"Ay mate, I'm glad to be back. I've had enough of it, to be honest! I just want to get back to my normal life, now. Although that's probably out of the question, the way the media is about this!" Jimmy said.

"Aye, well, you're a big star now, hey?...Oh!.." Tony said, looking down at the gift in his hands. "Everyone at work wishes you well, mate. and they got you this…"

Tony handed over a box of chocolates and a huge card that all the staff at work had signed.

"Ahhh! mate… that's so nice. Did you get everyone to sign it, yourself?" Jimmy asked, lightening up a little.

"Actually mate, it was Chloe in Accounts who bought it all." Tony said nonchalantly, just loud enough so Alice could hear," I think she's quite fond of you!" He added, whilst looking sideways at the kitchen.

Alice appeared in the door way with a huge overbite and frown. Jimmy looked flustered, as his eyes darted between Alice and Tony.

"Aye, well! It's very kind of everyone! Make sure you thank them for me, will ya, Tone?" He said whilst nodding his head, stoically.

Tony was enjoying watching Jimmy squirm and he wasn't finished yet.

"Yes, she seems very upset by it all! She said to ask you if it would be ok to meet up for a drink? You know just to see how you've been keeping."

James nearly spilled his coffee into his lap with this revelation, whilst Alice took a deep breath.

"HE WONT BE GOING ANYWHERE FOR A DRINK FOR A BLADDY LONG TIME ACTUALLY, TONY. HE NEEDS TO REST AND RECUPERATE . DONT YA, JIMMY?" She barked from the doorway, her strong Glaswegian accent suddenly shining through.

"Of course I won't, Hen. I wouldn't be going for a drink with her, anyway! I barely get out as it is!" Jimmy implored.

He wasn't prepared for this attack and he was on the ropes. Tony gleefully lapped up the scene, but decided to back off. He didn't want to make it too obvious he was stirring the pot on purpose.

"Aye, mate! Well...I'll tell her you'll be in touch later on, then, hey?.... Anyway, They reckon you're up for a George Cross, you know! The palace said they are considering it. They said its ok because technically we are at war with terrorism! Amazing that, mate! You must be dead proud!"

Tony was beaming and putting on his best friendly smile. Seizing the opportunity to change the subject, Jimmy jumped in.

"It's all a load of bullshit, Pal! I just did whatever any one else would do in the same situation. I wasn't out to catch any bloody terrorists! I was trying to get home for my dinner."

Tony gave a knowing nod.

"So come on mate, tell me what happened. I want all the juicy details, man!" He said, but Jimmy was in no mood to go over every detail again, and he was suddenly getting very bored of this conversation.

"Look Pal, if I'm honest, I'm still recovering and its been a long day, already. I was just asleep when you came in and I need to get my rest. I'll catch up with you later on in the week buddy, ok?"

With that, Jimmy ushered Tony back through the living room, down the hall and out of the front door, wincing every step of the way.

" Oh! Err…. SEE YA, ALICE!" Tony shouted, a little too keenly from the step.

"Yeah bye for now, Tony." Alice muttered under her breath, while she finished loading the washing machine. Silently, she was still fuming and frowned at Jimmy as he returned, slamming the washing machine door.

Chapter 17

Eyes closed. Only the sound of his breathing could be heard, and the ticking of the clock that cut the silence, into soft pieces of passing time. It had been a few days since his return home and James was drifting off to sleep again, when his meditation was smashed by the ring of the doorbell.

Alice answered.

"Well hello there! You must be Alice!" Nathan exhorted, as he grasped her hand.

"Ah yes. Nathan is it? Jayne said you would be calling around now. James is just in the living room. Hard to get him anywhere else at the moment! Even climbing the stairs to sleep is a chore."

"Hello again, Alice," said Jayne, as Alice led them down the narrow hall into the living room.

"Hi Jayne, I'm so glad to meet you properly, at last! Its always good to put a face to the voice on the end of the phone." She beamed.

Alice was on her best behaviour, today. All she could think about, was that hefty sum of money.

Jayne had noticed the family pictures pinned to the walls of the hall. The wallpaper was a tacky vinyl anaglypta, that Jayne wouldn't be seen dead hanging on her walls, but the pictures were cute. Holidays on some generic sunny beach, a sky diving photograph, a youth football team in black and white, a proposal on top of a mountain… Jayne made a mental note to ask about that. She was the last to walk in, just as Nathan was turning on the charm.

"Jamsie! Am I OK to call you Jamsie? So good to meet you, at last! No, please don't get up. You need the rest, big fella!" Nathan grabbed Jimmy's hand and frantically shook it, like a serial masturbator.

"Aye, well thanks for calling in, Nathan. Can we get you some tea?" James was a little overwhelmed. He was still a bit blurry eyed and tired from his, almost, afternoon nap.

Alice was already ahead of him and emerged from the kitchen with a teapot, four cups and a box of McVitie's Victoria biscuits.

"I planned ahead." She smiled as she set the tray down on the occasional table, next to Nathan on the couch.

"So, before we go any further Nathan, let's talk business. How are we gonna get paid for this story? I don't fully understand. Explain it to me like I'm 5 years old. Haha!"

James laughed a little awkwardly and hoped Nathan hadn't seen the small desperation in his approach.

He had.

"Well, as explained in the document you received before contacting us last week James, you will be paid an up front amount of £500,000 with an extra £500,000 on completion of three interviews. You will then be paid ad infinitum 20% of all income from online subscriptions, to read your story via our website. You will also be paid 20% of every licence to print the story globally, including hard copies and the Internet, that we sell to foreign news groups. You are, as of today, a very wealthy man, James!"

Nathan's Jackal like grimace stretched from ear to ear in a veiled smile. Fucking peasants. All they're bothered about is the money. Well they need to tow the line if they want the spoils, he thought, cynically. We are on mission from God, here!

"So, I'm assuming you'll transfer the initial payment after our chat, today? Call me old fashioned, but I trust no one these days. Haha!" James had his own veiled smile.

"Of course, Jamsie! I'll personally see to it at the end of today's session. So, down to business. We want to get a feel for who James McKenzie is. We are thinking everyday hero stuff. Family man pushed through extra ordinary circumstances, to become extraordinary himself. Like a super hero origin story, if you will. Ha!"

James snorted. What a load of bollocks, but I'll play his game.

"Lets start with your childhood." Said Nathan, as he produced a voice recorder, which he set recording and placed on the table.

" Well there's not much to tell to be honest, Nathan. I grew up in Hamilton, near Glasgow. I had a stable upbringing with my Maw and Paw. Played football through school and did some amateur boxing down the recreation centre on a Wednesday and Friday night.

I did pretty well at both, if I say so myself! Captained the local Harriers team to League and Cup glory through my teens and had a regional under 16 belt for the boxing, too!

I also loved to keep fit by walking in the mountains and that's how I met Alice."

"Oh, how lovely!" Jayne crooned. "Is that why you chose the mountain to propose?"

"Aye, that's right!" Said James. He was impressed with Jayne's attention to detail and also her beautiful long legs and short skirt.

"Tell us more, Alice. What's the background to this lovely romantic story?" Nathan probed.

"Well" said Alice, "Where do I start? I was in an athletics club in school and they always liked to walk up the mountains at the weekend. I think I was about 16 years old, still doing my A levels when the class climbed Tinto Hill, one Saturday afternoon. Jimmy was running down as I was going up and I fell into a little gorge because I was too busy eyeing him up! Hahaha! He saw me fall and came to my rescue. I asked him for his number and the rest is history, as they say."

Remembering this, was making Alice feel a bit warm inside. She had been so busy finding fault with Jimmy recently, that she had forgotten all the reasons why she loved him. She went over and gave him a cuddle from behind the chair. He winced a little, but grabbed her forearm and started to rub it gently with his thumb.

"Ah, that's so lovely! And what of the proposal?" Said Jayne. She was genuinely interested for a change.

"Ah well, James had left me hanging on forever! Haha! We were nigh on 23 and 24 before he proposed. He had kept me waiting and I was thinking he wasn't going to propose at all! I had told my sister, and unbeknownst to me, Jimmy had already bought me the ring! My sister said nothing of course and she let me go on believing he was a bastard, you know? Haha!

Anyway, James had organised a run up Ben Nevis for us, as I had a marathon coming up and I wanted to push my fitness. We made the summit in two and a half hours and then we stopped for a breather. James bent down like he was tying his shoe lace, but I thought he was injured! So I'm all 'James! You OK? Get up!' Trying to lift him to his feet, you know? Little did I know, he was laughing his head off, not crying!" Alice couldn't stop the giggles.

"He pulled out the ring but he couldn't propose because he was that hysterical with laughter! hahaha! "

Jimmy was trying his best not to laugh because it hurt so much, but he couldn't help it. His big guffaw followed by the wincing, gave everyone a laugh and Alice had to take a minute before continuing.

"Soo.. Anyway! We had a random guy at the top take our picture with James on one knee, still laughing our heads off. It was a moment." Alice looked him in the eyes and hugged him again, a little bit tighter this time. Jimmy looked up and smiled.

"So, 16 years married, now?" Jayne beamed, "and one beautiful son, Andy."

"That's right, he's round at a friend's, just now," Said Alice," He's extremely fond of you!" She playfully ribbed Jayne.

"Aren't we all? Haha!" blurted James. Much to the disdain of Alice.

She glared at him with her signature overbite, which only made an appearance when she was really pissed off. James shrunk a little into his seat.

Nathan was eager to move things on. He wanted to get to the juicy bits.

"Ah! that's lovely guys, anyway Jamsie, let's move on to the day that changed your life. Just walk us through it, will you?"

For a moment the room was silent apart from the ticking clock and James heavy breath. Nathan's voice recorder continued on.

"Well, Nathan. Things have started to come back to me a little more this past week. I'm dreaming of it now and it wakes me up. Bad dreams you know? I feel li...."

"Let me just stop you there, James. The readers are looking more for an account of the facts, at this point in the story. Just explain the events as they happened, hey?" Nathan was not interested in his namby pamby feelings! I can see this guys a fucking snowflake, he thought.

"Oh right... of course, yeah um... so what I remember... it was early evening... I was on the M56 coming home... Next thing I get hit from behind, the car fishtails... I end up flipping over. I get out... angry guy tries to hit me and my boxing kicked in. I floored him. Got shot by his brother, was it? " he looked at Alice who nodded, "I pulled out a few people from the wreckage, got blown up and then I passed out. " James was intentionally blasé in his rendition, giving as little information as he could. There was just something about this little prick that he didn't like.

Nathan sensed a little tension but was adamant on getting what he thought his readers wanted. He pushed on.

"So, it's become clear that the guy you knocked out and the man who shot you, work for a terrorist group called the Light of Mohammed. Have you heard of them?"

"Not really, Pal. Not very big on terrorists organisations, to be honest."

"Really? Ok well let me tell you, they are personally responsible for at least 5 major terrorist attacks in as many years, including the one in Manchester, where hundreds of your nation's men, women and children were killed or mutilated in that senseless explosion. How does that make you feel, James?"

Nathan was working into a slow fervour. James noticed the shift in tone and he didn't like it.

"Look, I'm disgusted as the next man about the senseless loss of life, not just in Manchester, but the world over through attacks like this, but come on, man! This country is asking for it, don't you think?"

Alice rolled her eyes and decided it was time to leave the room. Here goes James on another one of his major rants, again!

"Asking for it?...." Nathan genuinely didn't understand the comment, but felt a ball forming in his stomach. "What do you mean by that, James?" A dark frown settled on his brow.

"Well, you must see it, man! If the government of your country spends millions of tax payers money, buying weapons of mass destruction and then goes ahead and drops them on innocent kids in the middle east, just so they and their rich cronies can make a fortune in public contracts, you're asking for retaliation, aren't ye?

The problem is, the government are happy committing these atrocities, as they all have shares in, or sit on the board of the major players in arms and warfare. They don't care about the little people, and when I say that, I mean you and me, too! Not just these poor bastards in Afghan and other sorry hell holes we have created. All plays nicely into their hands, doesn't it? More terrorism means more budgets for defence which begets more draconian laws of surveillance in the name of security. People lose their freedom, but it happens slowly, eroding silently over time, so as not to stir up a revolt, and then one day, poof! You've suddenly got no rights at all!!"

James was red faced and breathing heavily. He was in pain with his wounds and sweating a little. Nathan was a weird mix of furious and bitterly disappointed in Mckenzie. He thought he was a Patriot, like himself! He thought he was fellow Christian who knew who the real pagans were! He was staggered.

"So...Would you go so far, as to not condemn these terrorists, James? Do you believe they have a right, or a cause worth fighting for?"

"No man! You're putting words in my mouth, just now. All I'm saying is, its understandable. What if it was you, or me? Or our Andrew?"

Nathan instantly thought of his brother and struggled to keep himself in check. Through gritted teeth he glared at James.

"I lost my brother in Iraq. I know how it feels and I know who's to blame." He spoke slowly and deliberately.

"Aw man, I'm genuinely sorry to hear that, Pal. I just think it's all so unnecessary and obscene. Aren't you bothered people are making money off this shit? Ask yourself, what did your brother actually

96

give his life for? Iraq has never had peace since the invasion. It's in a worse state than it was, beforehand! Likewise, in 10 years in Afghanistan there's nothing to show for it other than keeping the poppy fields secure! That's all I can see. It's a fucking crying shame, man!" James implored.

"My brother died defending his country, from monsters like the Khan brothers! I think we should terminate this interview here, Jayne. Let's reflect on what we have and we can take it up again with you another day, James."

Jayne quickly stood up and shook James hand.

"We'll be in touch." She said, with a thin smile.

Nathan stood and walked swiftly back through the front door and into the street. Jayne struggled to keep up with him as he marched over to his car.

As the front door slammed behind them, Alice shouted from the kitchen...

"Nice one, Jimmy! You well and truly fucked that one up!"

Chapter 18

A mir was bloodied and bruised and yet the main problem he had, was keeping his eyes open. He had no idea of the number of days he had been incarcerated. All he knew was the randomisation of beatings, questions and sleep deprivation, were starting to take their toll on his resolve.

He just needed to fall asleep so badly!

He was desperate to rest but as soon as his eyes closed, klaxons would sound, lights would flash on and off and men would rush in to beat him again. He had no idea how long it had been going on. He was close to breaking point and all the while that horrible voice in the background: Solomon Horowitz.

"Amir, we have a surprise for you today."

"Kol khara!" Amir breathed.

"Indeed, Amir. This is something we can visit soon, if you like? I am happy for you to eat shit, if it gets me what I want."

"Ayreh feek!!" Shouted Amir.

"I am impressed with your stamina, Amir. Your brother would be very proud, but it is futile and only prolongs the inevitable. We will discover all we need to know. It is God's will."

"I will never give you my brother! I WILL DIE BEFORE THAT HAPPENS!" Amir used up all his strength to punctuate the statement and flounced his head to his chest. Breathing heavily, with his arms spread wide and attached to the wall with handcuffs, Horowitz noticed how he looked like a picture of Jesus. His hair unkempt and his beard untrimmed, Amir looked haggard, sitting in his own filth.

"God's will is all, Amir and he wants you to talk. Like I said, we have a surprise for you, today. You have a visitor!"

With that, the double steel doors at the end of the cell flew open and two men dressed head to heel in black and wearing full face balaclavas, dragged a middle aged Arabian woman in to the room, by her hair. She was screaming and yet Horowitz saw how attractive she was through the contortions on her face. She stood about five foot six inches tall, with beautiful curves, olive skin and wavey brunette hair that would be below hair shoulders, had it not been scrunched painfully into the gloved hands of her assailants.

Amir cried out in fear, worry and sorrow. How did they find her?! How did they know?! A grimace of drawn lips and bared teeth, spread across his face. He was not expecting this.

Malika Noor was thrown to the floor in front of him.

He had met her at a family wedding in the Lebanon, two years previously. They had met in secret many times afterwards and developed a strong, beautiful relationship. They had kept it secret from both of their families and not even Aziz knew of their time together. She believed in the cause as much as he did, having seen first hand as a young girl, the brutality of the western influence in Beirut.

He loved her very much.

"Amir... Amir! Calm yourself." Horowitz laughed, enjoying the power of the situation. I will get what I want. I always do, he thought.

"You are not as invisible or untouchable as you think, Amir. You are always being watched. Did you think you could carry out these heinous crimes, anonymously? God sees all, Amir, as do your brothers in arms. It was in fact, your brother Aziz, who betrayed your love."

"LIAR!!!" Screamed Amir.

"No Amir, it is true."

It was a lie but Horowitz knew the power of undermining the bonds between family. His Mother's sister had witnessed the power of this approach in Belsen, when the Nazis had forced his grandfather to fuck her in front of the SS, in order to prevent her execution. These tactics were commonly used to break down the bonds of family and dehumanise the subjects. Horowitz planned something similar today.

"Amir, you have one chance to give up your team's location, or you may witness the worst hell for your love. We know your brother and his terrorist friends have not left the country, as every avenue for their escape has been closed. Please Amir, for Malika's sake and your own. Give us what we want."

Amir's head was spinning. There was no way he could give his brother up, but he might be able to save her, if he stalled this bastard with a fake address.

"OK! OK!! You win, I will tell you what you want to know."

"Begin...." Solomon ordered over the speakers.

"First, you must release Malika to her family and give me proof that she is safe, in their hands."

"Amir. You are confused as to who holds the power, here! Let me enlighten you... STRIP HER!" The speakers crackled.

The doors burst open again and some crudely formed wooden stocks were wheeled in sideways on to Amir's position. Three of the faceless men prepared it for Malika, whilst the original two, rudely stripped her of her clothes, slapping and beating her as they continued. All the while they were laughing and mocking her, as they screamed sexual obscenities about what they where going do to her, if Amir didn't talk. Amir was beside himself and screaming in frustration.

Eventually Malika sobbing and screaming was dragged to the stocks, where she was forced to kneel on the boards behind it. Her head and arms where padlocked into place whilst the men made crude noises and continued to mock and slap her, whilst she shivered naked and whimpering before them all.

"OK! OK! Please! Stop this insanity! I will tell you everything!"

"Better Amir, Better. Let's start with the address, please. Where are they located."

"Er.. erm... let me think, I..err, they are still in Manchester!" Amir was under serious pressure and he could not hide his lies well.

"Good now the address..."

"It's er 20 er Winchester Street in Leverhulme."

"YOU LIE!!" Screamed Horowitz.

One of the men seized a cat 'o' nine tails that had been place by the rack and began to flog Malika hard. There was a sickening crunch as the flails hit her beautiful olive toned body. The whip had been sown with stone knuckles, that felt like many fists punching her at once. She was screaming relentlessly, whilst the other men slapped her face and laughed.

"STOP! PLEASE STOP!" Wailed Amir.

"TELL ME THE LOCATION OF YOUR BROTHER! THERE IS NO SUCH STREET IN LEVERHULME!! TELL ME!"

"I cannot betray my brother," Amir whimpered as the tears scorched his cheeks.

"MEN!" Screamed Horowitz.

Over the next fifteen minutes, the five men descended on Malika, like depraved primal beasts. One forced himself into her rectum and thrust vigorously with his hips. On the end of his member, was a painful metal device of sharp cones that tore into the soft skin of Malika's insides. She screamed in terror and pain, as the other men continued to whip her and take turns in forcing themselves down her jaw locked throat. A simple dentist's cheek retractor had been put in place to stop her from biting down and perhaps seizing some small revenge.

"AZIZ' LOCATION NOW, AMIR! OR SHE DIES!" Insisted Horowitz.

"I'm sorry! I'm so sorry, Malika!" Amir, whimpered.

Amir was enveloped in utter desperation and sorrow. He sobbed, uncontrollably. It was all he could say, whilst the beasts continued their onslaught.

Horowitz knew Amir would not give up his brother in the face of this torture, if he hadn't done so already. This tactic was over. He entered the cell, walked calmly over to Malika and shot her clean through the forehead with his Beretta pistol.

Amir shrieked with all of his might, as his body shook and tears streaked his bruised and swollen cheeks. Instantly, grief and remorse consumed him. The shock of what he had witnessed manifested in a bitterly cold and dark fire, that raged through his body, flameless and yet all consuming in its destruction of his senses. All of their possible futures together, had been extinguished in an instant and the weight of that responsibility, turned his heart to dust.

Horowitz turned to face his quarry and what he said next terrified Amir so badly, that he pissed himself as the words were spoken.

"BRING IN HIS MOTHER."

Chapter 19

Y ou need to phone him back, you stupid bastard!"

Two days later and Alice was still furious. Not only had Jimmy completely fucked up the interview, but he'd also made a rash and embarrassing joke about how Jayne was sooo attractive! Right in front of her boyfriend and his own bloody wife! She was fuming.

"Alice, I'm not sure I even want to phone him back! What's the fucking point in selling your soul for money? I've known he was right wing press from the start, but I thought I'd have a chance to speak directly to his audience and maybe change a few views, eh, Hen?" Jimmy was deflated.

He knew that wasn't going to happen anymore and for all of the fantastic, patriotic hero worship the paper had done on his behalf in the first week, he had a bad feeling in his gut.

Maybe he should call Nathan back. See what he was planning to do.

"You can kiss goodbye to that fucking money, you dickhead!" Screamed Alice.

"What the fuck is going on with you, Alice? Is the money really worth falling out this badly over, or is it something else?"

"You fucking know what it is..." Alice seethed, as the overbite returned.

"For fucks sake, woman! I told ya! NOTHING HAPPENED BETWEEN ME AND CHLOE FROM WORK! For the final time, she had been spiked at the Christmas party and I took her safely upstairs to her room, so no fucking predator could get to her, for fucks sake! I put her fully clothed on the bed and she grabbed me and pulled me on top of herself, just as Judith from her department walked in. These fucking drugs make ya horny apparently and Chloe was seen by Judith, trying to undo my pants. Needless to say, Chloe was mighty fucking embarrassed the next day!"

Jimmy was red in the face and spitting.

"... But oh no! EVERYBODY loves a fucking scandal, don't they? So the next thing is, I'm getting the blame for spiking her, even though we BOTH FUCKING DENY IT!!"

He sat down hard into his chair and winced again. He was totally sick of being sick, now.

"If you don't believe me, just fuck off, will ye! I'm your husband and if there's no trust, there's no fucking marriage!"

Alice was taken aback.

"Right, you fucking prick! I'll go stay at my mother's, shall I? See how you cope on your own in the house without your fucking slave doing all the work! YOU can do your OWN FUCKING DISHES!!"

With that she stormed upstairs. Jimmy could NOT be arsed with this today and turned on the television. The F1 Highlights were just starting so he raised the volume especially loud. Upstairs, Alice was busy biting her nails.

That cheeky bastard! she thought. All I ever do is run around after him and Andy, and I get no thanks! He's right, though. Do I trust him? I just don't know if I can let it go, just in case he IS lying! Alice was in a quandary. Probably best if I do go to my mums for a bit, she thought. So, after packing a bag, Alice opened her phone and booked two train tickets North.

She stormed into Andy's room. He had his headphones on and he couldn't hear his mother shouting at him.

She ripped the head phones off his head.

"ANDY! I'M SICK OF SHOUTING TO TRY AND GET YOUR ATTENTION! Get a bag together. We are going to your Nanna's for a few days."

"Oh Mum! I don't want to go! I've got a tournament tonight on Twitch!" Andy implored.

"Don't fucking test me, lad! Get your shit together, now! The taxi will be here in 10 minutes. How would you like me to tell your Nanna that you refused to come and see her, over a fucking computer game? She would be heartbroken!"

Andy despondently collected his things in his rucksack, including his console. If he had to go to his Nan's, at least he would get to take part in the tournament later this evening.

James heard the taxi pull up and Andy shouted something from the hall. He must be going to his mate's, he thought, as the TV droned on.

Chapter 20

The bright hue from Tony's computer screen lit up his face, frowning in concentration. He hated the way the browser took so long when he was on the Dark Web. Obviously, it took time for the signal to bounce from the UK to Russia through Denmark and Greece and back again, before he could anonymously input his details to the vendor, but he always felt uneasy spending too long buying this shit.

Tony had used the last of his favourite product on the night of the previous staff party. He had stupidly been too impatient and administered the dose, way before he should have. If only he had waited another hour, he would have been in heaven! "Never mind", he thought. There's always next time.

He purchased some "GBL Alloy Cleaner" as quickly as he could and started a new hidden circuit on his "Tor" browser. He daydreamed a little whilst he waited for his favourite "Dark Web" chat site to load. Tony didn't like the word "Incel", he thought the Yanks were little cry babies and they should just take what they wanted, but he did agree with the views and opinions that he shared with them about women. He often visited these "Incel" chat rooms to brag about his conquests.

Tony had grown up in a violent household. His father was an alcoholic and had a chip on his shoulder, about how he thought his mother had tricked him into getting pregnant. Tony's Dad had always blamed his own failures in life on Tony's mother, and had systematically beaten, humiliated and raped her, in front of his young, impressionable son from an early age. His father would say things like, "This is all your mother is good for!" and "Women will take the piss out of you if you let them, lad! You have to put them in their place!" Tony grew up believing he was better than the women who refused him sex and believed it was his right as a man to take it, even if it wasn't freely given. His mind wandered back to Alice and Jimmy.

Usually he was just envious of the happy couple, but since he fucked up his plans with Chloe at the staff party, he was starting to hate him. He was so close to getting Chloe back to his room and getting to fuck her, but then Jimmy got involved like a goody two shoes and took her to her own room! Fucking prick. Jimmy had ruined Tony's whole night. Tony had no problem starting rumours about how Jimmy had spiked her. It was a great strategy. It threw people off the scent with him, and also made his hated Jimmy's life a little bit harder with Alice.

Ahhh, Alice.

Jimmy started to fantasise about being in her mouth. I can't wait for this batch to arrive, thought Tony. I just need my chance to be alone with her now.

Chapter 21

A mir's mother, Jamila Faruk, was born in 1946, in the coastal town of Naqoura in Southern Lebanon. Her father was so taken with his daughter's beauty, that Jamila was the only name he would settle on for his treasured daughter. By the time she was 30, at the start of the Lebanese Civil War, she had seen first hand the injustice and despair forced upon the Palestinian people by the formation of Israel in 1948. Tens of thousands of refugees had crossed the border and told tales of massacres, property theft and the destruction of whole neighbourhoods. The Nakba, had chilled her to the bone in her teenage years. She too, had witnessed the social and political instability created by a similar western "Mandate", that was forced on her homeland before she was born.

After France had withdrawn from Lebanon in 1946, peace ensued for a short time, until the pro Christian factions in power had started to monopolise industries and consolidate political power into their hands. This went against the post Colonial Lebanese Constitution, and so fighting had broken out in Beirut.

Jamila married a Palestinian refugee called Mohammed Khan in 1965 and they had decided to move to Beirut. They were happy until 1975 when they were caught up in the political unrest and both bore witness to the massacre in their home district of Quarantaine. Lucky to escape with their lives and forever traumatised by witnessing the rape and murder of friends and relatives, they decided to join Al Mourabiton. A pro Arab militia, hell bent on retaliation for the "Karantina" Massacre.

On January 29th 1976, fuelled by anger and hatred, they joined the force at Damour on the outskirts of Beirut, and helped massacre over 500 unarmed civilians in retaliation for "Karantina".

Together, they fought with Al Mourabiton and distinguished themselves helping secure West Beirut in the "Battle of The Hotels". Later they became disheartened with Al Mourabiton, as factional in fighting and misdirection took hold within their group and their allies. Jamila always blamed this division of her native brothers and sisters, as the critical reason why Lebanon had never seen social and political stability.

Aziz was born in 1970 in West Beirut and 8 years later, Amir in 78. They were a happy family as much as they could be in the circumstances and remained so, until 1981 when Mohammed was killed in a firefight with the Lebanese Front. After Mohammed's death and fearing for her son's safety, Jamila retired back to Naqoura to be with her family and gave up the life of violence.

She was always against the radicalisation of her sons by the PLO in Southern Lebanon, although she held no love for Christianity or the West. She just wanted to live in peace and wanted that for her sons too.

It was not to be.

Jamila was fighting off crippling fear and despair as she saw the battered and bruised face of her youngest. Her Prince. The contortions of pain and panic on his face only served to increase her desperation, as she hated seeing him in such anguish.

"LET HER GO!"

He screamed at Horowitz, as the faceless masks roughly stripped his ageing mother in front of his eyes. The degradation and humiliation! These demons have no soul! He raged inside, simultaneously feeling the futility of his situation and the embarassment of what he had bestowed on his "Mami" and his beautiful Malika. Still suffering from the traumatic shock of seeing his sweetheart raped and murdered in front of him, and now his mother, who must surely face the same fate if he did not capitulate, his head was reeling.

"Amir... Amir, listen to me. You can save your mother if you just tell me what I need to know. One way or another we will get the information we need, so why subject your dear mother to this humiliation? Her pain and yours will end, just as soon as you realise that you have no cards to play here. Give up the location of your brother and I will see to it that the judge in your trial knows you helped us. It will go well for you during sentencing." Horowitz lied.

His mother was bent over across the stocks and restrained, whilst one of Horowitz' dogs reeled in a glowing forge. In it, a white hot poker sat crackling, burning more brightly than any light Amir had ever seen. His eyes couldn't be any wider without his eyeballs popping out.

"NO!" He blurted.

"I will ask you one more time, Amir. Where is your brother." Horowitz took hold of the poker and slowly moved it around menacingly. It was already far too close to Jamila's naked back and she felt the heat from the scorched metal singe the small hairs at the base of her spine. Amir winced through gritted teeth.

" I do not know! I SWEAR TO YOU!" He knew his lie would not stand but he just could not betray his brother, even now!

Horowitz nonchalantly dragged the edge of the white hot tip down Jamila's naked back. She screamed and Amir cried out, as the seared flesh sizzled and the smell of his mother's burning skin, filled his nostrils.

"I PROMISE YOU AMIR, I WILL PUT THIS POKER DEEP INSIDE YOUR MOTHER IF YOU DO NOT SUBMIT YOUR BROTHER'S LOCATION!! WHERE IS YOUR BROTHER, AMIR!! DO NOT TEST ME!!"

Horowitz had learned how to feign anger early in his career. Along with a crazy look in the eyes, it helped his subjects to believe he was unstable and capable of anything. Of course he was very stable, and yet he was also capable of anything. Looking crazy and angry to his subjects seemed to help them understand this better. He was an excellent mimic of emotions.

He moved the poker slowly around the rear of Jamila. Her naked backside quivering and shaking with fear. She was still crying out in pain, the welts and blistering on her back were just starting to form.

"ENOUGH! ENOUGH! I will tell you everything, you bastard! Just let my mother go!" Amir was empty. He had nothing left to fight with and he had been broken. It almost felt like a liberation from this obscene situation. He felt such great relief tinged with unfathomable sadness.

" 'ana asf jidana ya 'umiy kulu hadha." Amir, in tears, apologised to his mother directly. Looking imploringly into her eyes, he never meant anything more deeply in his life. All Jamila could do was whimper and sob.

Within an hour of the information received from Amir, Horowitz' faceless agents stormed the house in Walkden, only to find an empty shell. Everything had gone, including Aziz and Abrafo. Forensics went to work on the building and its grounds, but nothing of any significance was found, just the body of an old Arab lady, murdered to keep her silent. Like the mist of daybreak, Aziz and Abrafo had vanished with the late morning breeze.

Chapter 22

James had fallen asleep again and hunger had woken him from a dark dream at 7.38pm. The house was quiet and Alice was nowhere to be seen. Strange, he thought. James winced in pain as he slowly rose from his chair and hobbled out into the hall.

"Alice… Alice!....ALICE!"

No answer. James was baffled. He began to go over what he remembered from this afternoon. He heard a taxi arrive around 4pm… hmmm and he remembered hearing Andy shouting something from the hall…

"Andy! are you home?!"

Still no answer. For fuck's sake! What's going on? He was not amused. He made his way slowly back to the living room where he noticed four missed calls on his phone. All from Alice. Fuck! He thought, are they OK?! He hit the speed dial button on his phone that was attached to her number.

"Alice are you OK? Where are you?" He sounded anxious.

"Ohh! So you do give a shiny shite about me, then?" Alice barked.

"For fuck's sake! I was worried then! Where are ya?"

"I'm staying with my mum for a few days. Andrew is with me. I think I need some time to decide what I want, James. You're right, I'm not sure I trust you anymore. Those rumours about you and that girl are everywhere and I..I just can't look at you at the moment."

"OK, my love. You take all the time you need."

James was livid but losing it on the phone wasn't going to help his situation.

"I'll be here when you decide what you want to do. I can't keep telling you the same thing and expect you to understand, if you're not listening. I've done all I can." With that, he hung up.

Alice and Jimmy had always had a tumultuous relationship. Ever since they had gotten together there was always tension. At first it was great because they worked it out through amazing sex. That's how Andy had come along. After the boy was born, things took a wrong turn between them. It was like all the love she had for him was suddenly redirected to the boy. He didn't mind at first because he was just as in love with their son as she was. He felt such joy and respect for her as a mother. He had always dreamed of this moment with her. Having a beautiful family unit that they could be proud of. Us against the world, he thought. Sure enough they had achieved that, but it seemed to be at the cost of their own relationship. It's like they had forgotten to be a couple and they were just parents, now. They hadn't been on a date for years. It made him sad to think about it. He loved her dearly, but they had drifted apart and the difference in their approach to life had become more apparent as the years went by. It seemed to James that all they did each day together, was argue.

"Right fuck this, I'm off the pub," He said out loud to himself.

25 mins later, he precariously climbed out of the cab and walked through the doors of The White Lion to tumultuous applause and cheering.

"Here he is! Our National Hero!" Said Ben, behind the bar.

The room erupted in a chorus of everyone chanting, "Gee Cee! Gee Cee!" James looked bashful and awkward.

"I hope you've come to drink! There's about two grand's worth of Tennant's behind the bar for ya!" Ben was laughing. People had been dropping by for two weeks and even calling the pub with donations for a pint.

"Aye lad, I'll take my first now!" Said James. There was a big cheer as they all bustled to shake his hand and give him a man hug.

"Watch it, boys! I'm still sore, ya know!"

James sat down with all eyes on him. He sat at the big table in the corner. Albert and Ronnie, the professional regulars, sat with him on either side, while the football lads settled in the gaps around them.

"How ya feeling, Big Man?" Ronnie said, with true concern on his face.

"I'm good Ron, how's yer sen?" James smiled.

"Come on, soft lad! tell us all about it, then!" Said Bert, as they all sat listening to the next rendition from Jamsie's lips.

By the time he had finished his story, he was more than a little bit drunk. Each time he had finished a few sentences, he was given a shot of tequila by one of the lads to keep the story flowing. He was smashed and he knew it.

"Right! The party's fucking started now, hey boys?!" He shouted as he stood up and started to wiggle his hips.

"Turn the fucking music up!" He demanded.

It was Bonnie Tyler. James loved a bit of Bonnie! He thought she was one of only a couple of wee singers, who could give him a good wrestle before sex.

"Fucking right, boys!" Jamsie shouted, as he waddled his hands up high to the sounds of Bonnie singing, "I NEED A HERO!"

"ITS FUCKING ME! YOU'RE HERO'S HERE, BONNIE LASS!" Jamsie blurted, as the pub fell about laughing.

Lapping up the attention, he noticed two younger ladies by the fire, both intently looking at him in a coy, sexy way. He couldn't be sure that was actually happening though, because he was that smashed. So, he decided to introduce himself and gauge the situation.

"Hello girls," he said in between hiccups, "not seen you here before?"

They both burst out laughing.

"Jimmy you soft cunt, it's me Shelley! from behind the bar! It's my night off haha!" she was hysterical.

"Och aye! My love… Christ! I didn't recognize you with your hair down and your make up on haha! how ya doin?"

"I'm good, Jimmy… this is my friend, Tasha."

"Hi, Tasha. Can I get yas a drink, then?" He slurred in his thick accent.

"Go on then, Jimmy, we'll have the same again. Ben knows what we have." Said Tasha with a sexy smile.

James returned to the bar and got two more Gin and Tonics from Ben. He was loving the attention from the girls. Still got it, ya old dog! He thought to himself.

"So what's it like being a big butch terrorist puncher, then?" Tasha said as she dragged her index finger up and down the strong muscles on James arm.

He had barely sat down between them and Shelley had put her hand high on his thigh. James was getting excited.

"Well someone had to do it, didn't they, Hen?" Jimmy laughed.

Both girls fell about laughing hysterically and continued the sensual touching. Jimmy had no idea he was so hilarious! He was beaming.

"Ah Jimmy, you're so funny!" Said Tasha, as she put her hand on his chest. "Let's have a dance." Shelley joined her and the pair of them pulled Jimmy to his feet.

The Bee Gees "Staying Alive" was playing on the Jukebox and Jimmy, wallowing in his new found fame, started throwing out some big moves. Unfortunately for him, the floor was wet from a few pint spills and he ended up flat on his arse with Shelley on top of him, legs flailing and her skirt riding up around her thighs. He grabbed out in his drunken state and felt her lithe backside. She giggled hysterically but made no attempt to stop him. Tasha pulled them both up and as Jimmy got to his feet, she grazed the front of his pants with her open hand.

Suddenly, Jimmy was getting very excited.

The dancing and flirting carried on for a while, until Shelley pulled Jimmy aside.

"Hey Jimmy, Tasha and I wondered if you wanted to invite us back to yours for a late drink after the pub shuts?" She twiddle the buttons on his polo shirt, while she stared into his eyes and smiled.

"Yeah! fuck it!" Jimmy blurted," Why the fuck not?"

He was really pissed off with Alice and he thought to himself, if I'm gonna be accused of this kinda thing, then I might as well do it! He pulled Shelley close by the base of her spine and whispered into her ear.

"Threesome?"

He thought he'd chance it, as he'd never had a threesome before, and this was an opportunity not to be missed with these incredibly sexy young women. Shelley just laughed and pushed her groin into his. Thirty minutes later they were in a cab heading home, leaving behind a lot of raised eyebrows in the pub.

In the cab, the girls were all over Jimmy. Both girls were taking it in turns to rub his crotch whilst he kissed them both with an open mouth. Very drunk and heavy handed, he was grabbing a breast here and there, and fumbling at their crotches.

Once in the house, he broke off from the girls and tried to play it cool.

"Can I get you girls a drink?" He slurred.

"Just take us to bed, you sexy bastard." Said Tasha in a mock Glaswegian accent and grabbed his dick in his trousers.

More kissing followed on the way up the stairs to his marital bedroom, as they fondled each other through their clothes. Half dressed, they all flopped on the bed.

The girls were all over him, kissing him sensually. Jimmy was totally in the moment, responding attentively to their lustful lips, swapping between them every minute or so. Shelley started moving down Jimmy's bare chest, kissing his nipples softly and making them hard with a soft bite between her teeth.

Tasha was busy stroking his hard member in his pants, whilst Jimmy released her warm, pert breasts, from her lacy, black bra.

Shelley continued to move lower, unbuttoning Jimmy's pants and taking them down, along with his underwear. Her breath quickened, as she stroked him and moved close enough to put him in her mouth.

Jimmy felt her move lower and started to breathe heavily. Then, in the midst of sucking on Tasha's tongue, he opened his eyes and over Tasha's shoulder, he caught a glimpse of his wife's photograph on his bedside table.

Instantly, he was racked with guilt.

What the fuck am I doing? He thought to himself and pushed the girls away.

"What's wrong, Jimmy?" Tasha said.

"Look, girls... I'm making a bad mistake here... we can't do this now. I love my wife. I'm sorry for fucking you about."

"For fuck's sake, Jimmy! We're not bothered! She won't find out! Just go with it. She will never know." Shelley laughed.

Jimmy sat up looking jaded and said,

"Aye Hen...She probably wouldn't know…

...but I would.

...Yas are gonna have to go. Now."

"Fucking hell, Jimmy!" Yelled Tasha, as both girls gathered their things and got dressed again.

They fumed in an awkward silence while they stomped down the stairs to the hallway. All the while Jimmy just looked at the floor, too embarrassed to lift his head and say goodbye.

"He must be fucking gay!" They joked, as they slammed the front door behind them, cackling to themselves.

Jimmy passed out on the bed.

The next day, James felt like Bonnie Tyler was trying to escape through his skull with a Lump Hammer. He thought he deserved that, after his bad behaviour the previous night. He did nothing that day except order takeaway, watch TV and miss his family. Very much. Outside, it was grey and raining.

Chapter 23

Sir George Rathbone received word from his operative in MI6, who was posing as "The Light of Mohammed's" anonymous benefactor, that Aziz was planning to kidnap the Mckenzie chap and use him as a trading piece for his brother, Amir.

He couldn't have been more delighted.

The Light of Mohammed had unsuspectingly been the tool of the Party's agenda for some time now. They had proven to be an excellent asset, however, there would be no negotiation or exchange.

Rathbone could see the glorious opportunity that lay ahead of him, and he knew he had to be careful in how he played it out. There could be no question of Rathbone's involvement in what happened next. MI6 could never know, as well as his own staff, not to mention the general public!

He set his plan in motion.

"We need to play this out carefully, David," Rathbone addressed the agent. " We need to extract McKenzie before they can get hold of him and keep him somewhere safe. Our middle eastern dogs are misbehaving and we cant have them running amok on their own vendetta!"

"I agree, Sir. We will move him and his family to a safe house until we can neutralise the cell, based on any future intelligence received from the Israeli." The agent was already tapping away on his tablet pc.

"Excellent, David. I shall leave it in your capable hands...May I suggest the house in North Wales? The location of the safehouse is close to Mckenzie and is currently available for occupation. Keep me informed of any updates." Sir George incepted.

"Right you are, Sir." replied David and he promptly retired.

Rathbone's mind was whirring. Already the fervour that had been stirred up over the incident was beyond what he could possibly have hoped for. There was a fantastic amount of fear that had been generated from the attack, and the press had done their best to enforce the idea, that all foreigners were suspect. It was exactly what he needed to win votes in The House, for the Sovereign Territories Defence Act. The vote was in a month's time and if he played his hand carefully, then the Act would be passed for certain.

Rathbone fixed himself a Whiskey. He opened the encrypted burner phone he kept a secret from everyone, including his wife and called a number.

"Nathan! How are you? ... good, good. I have another job for you, young man. I need you to interview our friend in the North one more time, but it's going to be a secret. I know it didn't pan out like we would have hoped last time, but that's fine. Something so much better has fallen into our lap and we can use it to our advantage. I will call with more specific instructions, when I know more. Pack a bag and be ready to go the day after tomorrow. Do this for me Nathan and I will see to it you're on the board of directors at the paper within a year. Who knows? Politics may be you're destiny, too. We need men like you, fighting the good fight!"

Cromwell puffed his chest out a little bit. "Thank you, Sir George. Always available for you, as you know. You know how much I appreciate what you've done for my career. My father sends his regards and says he will pop in for a visit before the vote."

"Excellent, my boy! I hope you'll be with him." Rathbone was grinning.

"Of course, Sir George. I'm looking forward to it."

Nathan hung up. What's the old fella up to now? He pondered.

Chapter 24

Aziz and Abrafo had to assume that Amir had cracked sooner rather than later. It had only been a few days since his capture and yet, as much as his brother loved him, he knew that eventually he would give up everything he knew. Everyone says that they could withstand torture, and yet getting absolutely no sleep for just two weeks, will bring a man to his knees for just five minutes rest.

They had decided to clear the house in Walkden the day Aziz formulated the plan to kidnap the Khalet. That would no doubt be the first place to be raided. After considering all the options, they had murdered their house keeper, Manal, the only person to have contact with them after the attack, and decided to steal a white long wheel base transit van. The duo had been living in the back of the stolen van since they left Walkden.

They had taken all of their necessary equipment with them. It had been the safest option. A simple change of Registration plates would be enough to give them anonymity, as long as they stayed away from built up areas and the ever present CCTV, and ANPR on the roads. There were so many white transits in circulation that they could easily escape detection. All that was needed was a set of different plates and a syphon to steal fuel at night. Aziz felt that they would be safer out on the road moving from place to place. The less contact they had with the general public, the better.

Currently, both men were staking out the Mckenzie house from a safe distance. Aziz was looking at the rear of the house from a farmers field, with a night vision sight that was attached to his old, Zastava M70 assault rifle. As they were in enemy territory, sourcing weapons had been difficult. Especially in the UK, where the gun restrictions were very excessive. The unit had decided a while ago to keep an arms and ammunition stash close to operations in case of emergencies such as this. The M70 is a variant of the Russian made Kalashnikov assault rifle. Celebrated the world over for its ingenious and simplistic design, the Kalashnikov was a always safe and reliable choice for the Arabs.

Abrafo had the same weapon to his left as he peered through his night vision goggles, assessing the cul de sac from behind the drivers seat of the Transit van. He was parked a little to the left of the cul de sac, on the main road opposite. They had been there for some time.

Aziz broke the silence on the encrypted short wave radio.

"Any movement at the front?"

"No, Sir. The lights are on, but I see no shadows or movement."

Abrafo hated stake outs. He needed to keep his mind busy all the time, otherwise he made mistakes. Patience was not his forte. He looked away to concentrate on the road ahead and behind. Forever mindful of their situation, he was always prepared for an ambush. There were two cars that were on his radar. Both Fords and both had been there for two days without moving. Not particularly suspicious but worthy of note, he thought.

"The more we see no change the more suspicious I am, Abrafo. Something doesn't feel right."

"I agree, Sir, but we need to know if he's in there."

Just then, a taxi pulled into the cul de sac and stopped in front of the Mckenzie house. The Nadhl's wife and son! But where is he? Thought Abrafo. He was getting restless. He watched as the taxi driver unloaded two small cases from the boot of the car. The brat took them, while his bitch mother opened the door.... But was the Khalet home?! No sign in the hallway, from what he could see.

It had originally been decided by the top brass, that a team of agents would wait at the Mckenzie house, to ambush any attempt by the insurgents at kidnapping the family. The MI6 agent who was in charge of the ambush, got a signal on the radio to break cover and approach the Mckenzie family in order to evacuate them. Apparently, the plans had changed. He thought this was odd. If the bastards were watching the house, it would be better to neutralise them here, than let them escape! He thought. However, not one to challenge his orders, he broke cover and knocked on the door.

"Mrs. Mckenzie? Hello, Ma'am. I have been instructed to collect you and Andrew and move you to a secure location. It has come to the attention of the government, that you are both in imminent danger from the terrorist cell that attacked your husband two weeks ago. Bring your cases and follow me, please."

Alice was taken aback. The anxiety was like a great black wave that crashed on the rock in her stomach.

"Where is James? Is he OK? Will we be with him?"

Just then Tony came crashing through the back door, as per usual.

"Hi gang! How's my favourite family?" He said, grinning from ear to ear. The agent drew his side arm so rapidly, that Tony jumped back and squealed.

"Who are you? State your business!" Shouted the agent.

"He's just the neighbour!" Blurted Alice.

"Sir, I am going to have to ask you to come with us. I believe the house is being watched by a terrorist cell, and you will no doubt become a target for interrogation and possible execution. It's best that you come with us. Now."

"What?..." Tony was puzzled, " err, I need a few things from the house if I'm staying away."

"Hurry, Sir." The agent said," You have three minutes."

As was stated, within three minutes Tony, Alice and Andrew were travelling at high speed to an undisclosed location, and Abrafo and Aziz were long gone into the darkness.

Chapter 25

James McKenzie sat bewildered in a strange house, thinking about the last six hours. He had been rudely awakened with a banging on the door at six o clock in the morning. He was met by four agents in full tactical gear and a fifth man in a suit, who explained that he was in imminent danger from the same lads he had run into on the motorway. They had whisked him away in his pyjamas, with very few things in his rucksack. Just a change of clothes, some deodorant, his razor and a comb was all he could think to pack in the three minutes they had given him to prepare. They had driven west along the M56, then in to Wales on the A55 and had turned off onto the A494. They had taken a scenic route through the Denbighshire hills, passing through the small towns of Bodfari and Trefnant. They finished their journey at an old stone house, opposite a beautiful Church with a stunning steeple, in a quiet village he had never heard of before.

James had been taken aback by the unique cladding of the church. Time and traffic had turned the once beautiful white stone a little grey, but its beauty was still unquestionable. Although the safe house was almost parallel with the A55, as it wound around the North Welsh headlands, it was still nice and secluded. No one would be thinking of looking for him here, he thought.

The agent in the suit, who had introduced himself as Jake, had told him to make himself at home. There was cable TV and a game system, books on the shelves and even a small Gym in one of the rooms. James surmised that whoever gets stashed here, is usually here for some time. It didn't make him feel good. Jake had explained that Alice and Andy would be picked up as soon as they came home. They had contacted her mother and she confirmed that they were already on the train heading South. He had tried to contact Alice but the reception was terrible, a common issue on the British railway system. He was now resigned to the idea, of waiting for Alice to call him. He couldn't wait to see them, but he had been told they wouldn't get moved to the same location as him, because they didn't want to risk keeping the family all in the same place. It was standard protocol with high value assets, they said. Jimmy didn't feel high value at all.

Jimmy hadn't eaten since yesterday dinner time and he was starving.

"Hey Jake, any chance of getting something to eat? I'm fading away here." He said with a big friendly smile.

" Of course, Sir." He addressed one of the other agents, " Dan, could you throw a few pizzas in the oven for us all?"

"Sir."

'Dan' left for the kitchen, whilst 'Jake' stood by the window peering through the blinds.

"You know, it was a heroic thing you did there Mr. McKenzie, at great risk to your own life. If it was up to me, you would definitely have that George Cross. You have my respect."

Jimmy shifted uneasily in his seat.

" Well, thanks Jake, but I was just doing what I think anyone would do. Those people needed help otherwise, they were gonna die." He said.

James reached inside his jeans pocket and took out his mobile. He was checking for messages from Alice, just as it started ringing. It was Nathan Cromwell from the paper again. Jimmy was intrigued.

"Hello Nathan, How are you?"

"Jimmy! I'm good my man! Listen… I've been thinking and I just wanted to apologise for my outbursts at our last meeting. I was totally out of order arguing with you. I've come to realise it's not my place to offer my opinion. The article should be about how you feel."

"Well… that's a U-turn I wasn't expecting, Nathan."

"Don't think of it so much as a U-turn, more of a delayed understanding of your truth. I was hoping that you would like to continue with our three part feature?"

"Well, obviously I'd love to, but it's not as simple as that, Nathan."

"Ah yes, of course. I heard on the grapevine you have recently took a vacation? Shall we say? Haha! I have a lot of contacts in the intelligence community, James. I have it on good authority, that you are currently a target of revenge by the same bastards that attacked you on the motorway."

Jimmy was taken aback. Bloody hell! He must have friends in high places and if he knows? Who else knows? He started to feel cornered.

" Listen Nathan, I don't know where you got your information from, but you have to swear that you and your source will remain…"

" James, I'll stop you there… Don't worry I have no idea where you are so you have nothing to fear, your location is completely confidential, however… I just can't resist asking you for a juicy little interview on how you feel right now. It's media gold, my friend! A face to face meeting with you would definitely be worth more to the paper. We will be happy to add £500,000 to our initial offer, if you're willing to do it?"

Christ! Thought James. £1.5 million big ones for just three interviews!

"Right, ok Nathan. How do we go about doing it, then?"

"Well don't you worry about that just yet, my friend. I will speak to my contacts and see if we can get to you over the next day or so. We will be in and out before anyone knows. Of course, we will be hooded so your location will remain confidential. We could have done the interview by phone, but I'd prefer it if we could get some photographs with you, just to add to the tension and give a little credence to the report."

" Right, ok. Sounds good to me. Call me when you know more."

James hung up. Let's hope they catch these bastards quickly, thought James. He was already thinking about spending the money.

Chapter 26

Alice, Andy and Tony had been brought at great speed and under an armed guard, to an undisclosed location in the Peak District. They had not been taken to the same place as Jimmy for "security reasons" and all the shouting in the world had not helped Alice overturn that decision.

They had each been given a separate room in the three bedroomed house. The perimeter was being watched front and back, by two agents and three more had took up residency in the rooms down stairs. They were relieved every six hours, so there would always be someone awake to protect them. Alice, Andy and Tony were gathered in the living room watching the television. One agent was in the kitchen and another was watching the street through the window blinds. The final agent could be heard moving around upstairs.

The twenty four hour news channels had been following the story on James for the last forty eight hours. The anchors and their respective guests had been debating the rights and wrongs of the Sovereign Territories Defence Act and the need to lock down the borders. The general tone of the chat was one of fear mongering. Whilst the commentary had been passionate and very heated from the pundits, Alice noticed it was only on the very specific subject, of how the last terrorist attack should encourage more draconian security measures for everyone.

"I need a drink." Alice groaned." Do we have anything in the house?" She said to no one in particular.

The agent came in from the kitchen and bent down, whispering.

"We aren't supposed to have stuff on the job and we aren't supposed to let you drink, but in the circumstances, I think a few would be OK. Just don't get hammered, in case we have to leave quickly." He gave a nod and a wink then produced a bottle of wine that he had taken from one of the kitchen cupboards.

For the first time in a week, Alice grinned.

"Excellent!" She said "Tony, you having one?"

"Yeah, sure!" Tony said and smirked.

Andy rolled his eyes, and left for the temporary respite of his new room to play games on his phone.

After a few gulps, Tony tested the water.

He knelt into Alice and whispered, " Hey, do you wanna go upstairs and get away from the ear wigs? The news is depressing me, anyway!"

"Yeah, come on," Alice said. She was truly bored of the news, too. She worried about James, but all of this fear talk was making her even more anxious for his safety.

The two went upstairs to Tony's room. Alice sat in the chair by the window and Tony lay back on the bed.

"So...How are you doing, Alice?" Tony asked, feigning interest.

She sighed heavily. "I'm not good, Tone. Everything has just been a little bit crazy lately, you know?" Tony gave a knowing nod.

"James has been a horror these past few months. Always arguing with me over petty things. He's very pissed off with me over this thing with the girl from work! Making it out that I'm crazy for thinking something was going on, when the facts speak for themselves!"

" Yeah... all looks very suspicious, if you ask me." Tony lied, "Everyone in work thinks he done it, you know."

"Do they?? Oh god! Tone! I don't know what to think!" Alice looked pained. "I still think I love him and all this has made me realise that. I think we need to have a proper sit down and talk it out."

"That's the best you can hope for I reckon, my love."

Tony was playing the part. He was getting hard, excited about the risk he was taking and imagining what might be coming next, if only he could just get a window of opportunity.

"He even thinks there's something going on between me and you! Ha!" Alice laughed, "I mean, come on! Imagine that?!" She looked at him with a daft look on her face.

Cheeky bitch, he thought. You'll be laughing on the other side of your face, soon.

"Haha, imagine that, hey?" He sneered back at her, but she didn't notice. She was in her own bubble and feeling a little tipsy now.

"I need the loo," she said and left the room for the bathroom.

Tony took the opportunity.

He moved swiftly. Taking the vial out of his pocket, he used the attached dropper to mix 4 drops of the clear, tasteless liquid into her drink. 1ml exactly. Just enough to cloud her mind and make her feel horny enough to go along with it, he thought. He heard the toilet flush and deftly returned to the bed, as if he hadn't moved an inch.

Alice returned and sat in the chair.

"I hope Jimmy's OK, wherever he is. I'm really worried." She put her head in her hands and started to weep.

"Ahh there there, darling."

Tony moved to the end of the bed to comfort her.

"I always think it's best to have drink in these situations, hey? Calms the nerves."

He pushed the glass to her lips and she took a big swig.

"Let me fill that for you," He said.

He was getting harder with each moment. He loved this part. Watching them go from being in control, to a glaze around the eyes and then HIM being in control. The rush was like nothing else.

He filled her glass again and she took another gulp. They spoke for a further 20 minutes, or so. Chatting the inevitable bollocks about how they should work through this bad patch and try and keep the marriage together. Tony was getting impatient and bored.

"I just wish it could all go back to how it was when we were younger, you know? Without all the bickering and mistrust. I do love him, he just winds me up so much!" She said whilst taking another drink.

Tony just sat back and nodded. Waiting.

Alice eyes started to droop a little and her head started to lol left and right on her shoulders. She was slurring her words and started to forget to finish her sentences.

"Bloody hell... I feel...." She garbled and then she was under.

Tony moved like a winged vampire, gliding to her chair and grabbing her face. He kissed her and as they always did, she responded. She was so disassociated she probably thought it was Jimmy, Tony realised, and it gave him a rush. Finally she was his!

He took the drink from her hand as she sat there limp, then he unbuttoned her blouse and pulled it down behind her back. She was restricted and he liked that. She tried to grab for his crotch, but he moved around behind her.

He leaned her forward and fumbled with her bra, just managing to get it undone. Alice's perfect breasts fell from the brazier and Tony felt a rush of adrenaline, as he caressed them and teased her nipples with his fingers. He gave them both a very hard pinch between his fingers, just to test her reactions. His member filled with blood as he did this, wallowing in the power over his hapless victim. She barely winced and he knew she was ready.

He lay her down on the bed and lifted the skirt of her summer dress, revealing black lacy panties. Tony rolled her sideways, to try and clear the skirt from her hips. He dragged each side up and over her curves, enjoying how she was a dead weight. Easy meat, he thought and rolled her onto her back again. He couldn't contain his excitement as he half pulled down her panties and then dropped his own pants. He mounted Alice on her chest and began to drag himself across her face. Alice responded by trying to put him in her mouth, but Tony pulled away. Not yet bitch, he thought. I want you from behind first. Tony got back to his feet with his pants around his ankles and tried to turn Alice over on the bed.

To his horror, she kept on rolling as he fumbled to catch her and tripped over his own pants around his ankles. Alice smashed her head on the table. She groaned and tried to stand up but tripped on the table leg. She didn't have the where with all to even put her arms out and face planted onto the floor, hard. He rolled her over and her forehead and nose were bleeding profusely. Fuuuuck!! Tony panicked.

Within seconds, three agents had barged into the room, expecting a surprise attack from insurgents. Andy swiftly followed and saw Tony, desperately trying to re-button Alice's blouse, still with his pants round his ankles. It was immediately apparent what had happened to Andy. The anger exploded inside him and he leaped at Tony, fists flying. He got three good digs into the bastard's face, before being torn away by one of the agents.

"You fucking dirty bastard! I'LL FUCKING KILL YOU!" He screamed, as he was dragged out of the room.

"Listen! She was really drunk and coming on to me before she fell and hit her head! Honestly, man!" Tony whined as he was being cuffed to the radiator.

"Let's see what she says when she wakes, hey?" The agent said whilst picking up the wine and smelling it. He could smell nothing untoward and yet he was still not satisfied.

"Empty his pockets." he told another agent.

Tony protested, but it was to no avail. They discovered the vial and saved the wine for testing. The next day, Alice and Andrew were on their way to another safe house and Tony was arrested on suspicion of a serious sexual assault. Alice, Andrew and the agents, would later give evidence that would see Tony charged and convicted.

He was forced to sign the sex offenders register for life on his release from prison. Everyone knew it was him who had drugged Chloe at work, although it couldn't be proven. Unemployed and penniless, Tony was a ruined man.

Chapter 27

The heavens had opened the moment the mini convoy had left Manchester Airport. Nathan Cromwell hated the North. Always fucking pissing down! Full of dense dickheads who only had themselves to blame for being poor. If half the beggars on the streets put as much effort into getting a job as they did trying to fleece him, there wouldn't be any homelessness! He mused.

Nathan's ex girlfriend Emma, said that he was blissfully unaware that the construct of a Capitalist Society by its very nature, needs poverty in order to sustain itself. The very concept of profit, means that there is always someone below you on the economic pyramid, being robbed of the true value of their time and labour. Inevitably, those at the bottom will suffer, when trying to access imperative resources, like food or housing, without the money to do so. Nathan's 'Ex' also believed that there was enough money and property around the globe, to house every homeless person in every country. Yet homeless people were on the rise, everywhere. Nathan couldn't understand her point of view.

She believed that homelessness was by design and not an unsolvable problem created by loafers and freeloaders. She was always yapping on about how the homeless were there to scare the working poor in to employment. It was a great tool for the Ruling Class. It helped motivate the working class to work in terrible conditions for little or no money. A cold, stark reminder that if they didn't capitulate, then it would be them on the streets, shivering under cardboard blankets. Nathan shuddered at the thought of Emma's whiny voice, droning on. I'm glad that relationship didn't last long! He scoffed.

He just thought poor people and the homeless were lazy.

His phone was buzzing in his pocket and so he answered it.

"Sir George, how are you?" He gushed.

"Very well, Nathan. I trust your flight was short and sweet?....So listen, I need you to make sure that you get some photographs with our man. Some inside for the paper and some outside in the front garden, facing due east. It's very important that you take the photographs due east, my boy."

Nathan was a little bewildered, but agreed to the strange demand.

"Do we try to steer his perspective towards our objectives today, Sir?"

"What an excellent idea!" Rathbone announced, as if he hadn't thought meticulously about this before.

"If you could get him to talk a little on the Sovereign Territories Defence Act, that would be fantastic Nathan. Steer him towards an approval, as much as you can. I know he's a slippery fish my boy, but I have full faith in your abilities. This will help us immensely in the coming weeks, to get the Act passed in The House. He has the weight of public opinion at the moment, so what he says is of enormous importance. You know, your father and I have worked tirelessly behind the scenes, to get this Act passed in your brother's name, Nathan. Your brother's sacrifice will not be in vain. You have my word."

Rathbone could always deflect Nathan's prying nature, by mentioning his brother. He was an easy puppet to control.

"Yes, Sir." Nathan felt a surge of determination to do well. "Thank you, Sir George, I won't let you down." He ended the call.

As the blacked out SUV made its way along the A55, Nathan was given a hood. He nonchalantly put it over his head and it wasn't long before the vehicle slowed and exited the main road. It was a short two minutes to the safehouse from there. Nathan thanked the driver as he removed the hood and waited until the car left, before approaching the door. He knocked and entered, walking past 'Jake'.

"Jamsie! How are you, my friend?"

Nathan strode towards James with his arms wide apart before vigorously shaking his hand. James was starting to hate the way he used "Jamsie" as a pet name. Only his friends called him that and a friend, he was not.

"Good, Nathan. Thank you for asking. Just a little put out by all of this, you know?"

"Ah yes, my friend. Its a dire set of circumstances, for sure. I understand you haven't seen Alice and Andy since this development. Have you talked on the phone?"

"Not yet. It's been a while, as she has been to her mother's for a visit. Seems like there's no signal where she is."

"Well, maybe these guys can do something about that, hey?" He said, waving his arms vaguely at the agents. "Anyway, I won't risk being here too long. Let's get down to brass tacks."

Nathan took off his coat, sat down and produced the familiar sound recorder that Jimmy had seen at the house.

"Jayne sends her regards. She had a family event today, so she couldn't make it." Said Nathan.

In reality Nathan hadn't disclosed where he was going to Jayne. It was Nathan's opinion, that the fewer people who knew about the visit, the better for all involved. Besides, It wouldn't look good to the security forces, if he brought her along. Sir George had said he'd pulled a lot of favours to get Nathan there already, so Jayne was a no go.

"Ahh, tell her I said hello when ya see her," James said with a smile. She was so beautiful. Beautiful women always made him smile.

Nathan started the recorder.

"So James, how have things been in the last few days?"

"Well things have been hard on the family, Nathan. We've been split up by this whole debacle and we have had no contact, so obviously, I'm worried and scared for them and myself."

"Yes, it must be frightening for you. Tell me about what happened after you heard of the threat from the insurgents to kidnap you."

James spoke at length about the extraction from the family home and how they came to be there. Being careful not to mention anything in specific detail.

"Wow that's some story, hey? When do you think this is going to end, Jamsie?"

"I'm hoping it's going to end very soon! I've been talking to the lads here, and they say they have some leads to follow up on these terrorists, so hopefully they will be caught as soon as possible and we can all go back to some semblance of normality, hey?"

"Indeed James, indeed. These devils will stop at nothing to attack our freedom and democracy!" Nathan said passionately.

Oh here we go! Thought James, but he held his tongue, as he didn't want to rile Nathan and chance losing the money.

"Aye, well. They certainly seem out of their minds, that's for sure."

The interview went on and they talked about how this wasn't going to upset the families plans for the future, how they wouldn't scare him and how the "Great British Resolve" would win out in the end. James knew Nathan was leading the conversation down a passive Nationalistic route, but he was tired and all this had knocked him. He no longer had the verve to argue, and so he let Nathan flow.

"So James, with all of the furore over the attack a few weeks ago, it seems very timely that the Sovereign Territories Defence Act is being passed through Parliament. What are your thoughts on this?" Nathan did his best to look interested.

"Well, the cynic in me would say that its all very timely, indeed!" James laughed, sardonically. However, after reading the room, his grin quickly faded to a grimace.

"What I mean is, the conspiracy theorists would say that, maybe they are related in some way? Governments have been known to use false flag deceptions before, have they not? ... er... I'm not saying that this is happening of course but er...well, scratch that Nathan, er let's start again."

James thought how this might sound to the families of the victims and decided it was in bad taste, even though he half thought it might be true. Nathan nodded his head and offered an outstretched palm, as if to say continue.

"Look, we've had the conversation before, haven't we? The root of the problem lies in the obscene way that the war machine makes money, blowing wee kids to bits in foreign lands, mixed with the outright theft of valuable resources within these lands, by faceless corporations who control the decision making, through buying off the politicians.

Terrorism is a symptom of that obscene process.

I truly believe that this Act and the consequences of it, will mean less security for the average man and more surveillance on the public by the powers that be. Travel will be a nightmare and we will lose valuable, specialised labour, needed for the economy here, due to the draconian measures on immigration that are written into the fabric of this Act of Parliament. It seems to me, that this fear mongering will cause yet more separation and isolation from the world stage and from each other, as human beings.

However, if we could stop the war machine, then we could watch the world heal itself from terrorism for good."

Nathan had stopped listening half way through and was admiring one of the agent's semi automatic Glock small machine guns, from afar. He came round, just at the right time.

"Yes, well, you are entitled to your opinion, of course. Right, I think we should break for lunch." Nathan was getting hungry.

Around one o'clock in the afternoon, a small finger buffet arrived from a local cafe. Nathan seemed happy with the interview and was ready for some photographs.

"Just to prove we have actually interviewed you whilst you're incognito, we need a few photographs for the story. Maybe a few inside and a couple outside?" He said.

James agreed and posed for a few photos with his agents. Nathan explained the agents faces would be blurred out. It would make the interview look authentic and add a little sensational drama. Both excellent selling points to the consumer.

"OK guys, I'd like take a few outside in the garden to show that James isn't scared and is relaxing in his new environment. Just to back up the Great British stiff upper lip vibe!"

They moved outside. The agents eyes furtively scanning the area for signs of danger, whilst James followed Nathan. In the garden was a set of outdoor furniture, ideally facing west to catch the setting sun. Perfect, thought Nathan. He got James to sit with the sun on his face.

"That's great, Jamsie! Just sit back with your hands in your pockets looking into the distance, like you haven't got a care in the world." Nathan said as he happily snapped away with his camera.

Afterwards, on the flight back to London, Nathan was scanning the photos. Still none the wiser as to why Sir George needed a photograph looking due east, all he could see was a swing in the garden and the tall spire of the local church in the background, shining like a bright grey beacon in the afternoon sunshine.

Chapter 28

The Mongoose could not believe his luck! He had just gotten off the phone with his mysterious benefactor and somehow, amazingly! they had found out the location of that Nadhl, Mckenzie! Oh! Allah shines on us! He thought. He allowed himself to have a little daydream about seeing his brother again and being rid of this rainy, grey island for ever!

They had been given an address for their target in a quiet village somewhere in North Wales, close to the motorway and with plenty of wilderness in which to make their escape. This is perfect, he thought. It would take some planning and time was of the essence. Aziz believed that every day Amir was imprisoned, meant a day closer to his execution. He just wanted him back and in one piece.

"Abrafo, pull up the online map of North Wales. We need to plan the extraction and look for a suitable place where we are safe to hold him."

"Allah will provide, my brother! Let's scout the area for a derelict building or a remote barn. Hopefully we can extract him and hold him there for a day or so. It shouldn't take too long for these bastards to comply."

Abrafo got busy with searching the area for some possible sites, whilst Aziz concentrated on the extraction. He pulled up the address of the safe house in Bodelwyddan and entered the street view. There was a lot of open space around the house with a good cover of vegetation, immediately across the road in the local church. This was good news. It would make a stakeout much easier. Mckenzie's protectors are highly trained and it was imperative that they remained hidden, to ensure the element of surprise.

Aziz thought back to his time with the PLO in South Lebanon. According to his superiors, Aziz was highly intelligent, very motivated and the most passionate about the cause. These qualities proved to be the reason that he had always been singled out for specialist training. He had learned many skills and tactics associated with guerrilla warfare, which included assassination techniques and the art of Kidnap.

He remembered that when stalking a foe, you will always have an advantage if you can recognise a routine. Routine gives you an opportunity to land a strike when your enemy is at its weakest. It could be a change in shift, or a newspaper delivery etc. Anything that can be predicted to happen again, is a weakness to exploit.

Aziz was a master at finding weakness.

They set off for North Wales in the van, sticking to the smaller roads and staying away from the areas most likely to have ANPR. They followed a similar route to the one James had travelled just days before.

They reached Rhuddlan Road around 6pm and decided to park in the local 7-11 car park, just a few minutes walk from the house. They got in the back of the van and made themselves useful, cleaning their weapons and checking the kit. Aziz planned a stake out of the house, for at least a few days, to glean any daily routines that he could make use of. Abrafo would take the opposing shift to Aziz and in this way, they had the house under surveillance at all times and they could both rest when needed. Both of them had full "Ghillie" suits; extreme camouflage, all in one body socks, that rendered the wearer practically invisible to the naked eye. Staying out of sight shouldn't be a problem. There's a small possibility that they could have heat seeking cameras, although their benefactor had assured him this wasn't the case.

After dark and the close of business, the town was quiet. Like snakes, the soldiers slid out of the Transit and moved silently into position to watch the house.

Abrafo immediately tried to sleep and Aziz took the first shift. Nothing of interest happened through the night, other than the front left hand bedroom light remained on until around 11.30pm. Downstairs, the lounge had a light on all night and the light of the room next door, came on at midnight and again at 6am. This suggested that Mckenzie was sleeping upstairs and the agents where next to the lounge, covering two six hour shifts a day. How many agents were present was yet to be ascertained.

Aziz woke Abrafo at 7am and told him what he had discovered. He then fell asleep in the cold. Throughout the day, Abrafo noted that James came outside for around 15 mins to eat his lunch at 12.30pm. He drank what looked like coffee and then returned inside the house. Abrafo noted with disdain, that he was forever under the watchful eye of two of the agents. This suggested to Abrafo, that there was at least four agents present, as the house would need to be covered, front and back, whilst the agents were outside. He noticed that although the agents were watchful, they were very relaxed. Not aware of any imminent danger, thought Abrafo. This is good.

At around 5.45pm an agent left the house and walked down to the coffee shop by the 7-11. Abrafo watched him walk back ten minutes later with five coffees. Four on a tray and one in his hand. Including James, this was a reasonable indication that there were four agents in the house. Abrafo was pleased. He thought that the odds of success were very good with only four agents. At 7pm he woke Aziz and told him the good news. Soon afterwards, he was asleep.

The only objective left was to try and glean the interior of the house. This was not easy. Aziz broke cover in the early hours and scouted the rear of the building, picking his way through the neighbourhood wearing his infra red night vision goggles and jumping into the neighbours gardens to the rear of the property. He took his time, moving from cover to cover, so as not to raise any alarm. He eventually scaled the wall to the rear of the building and waited in the dark shadows of a bush, scanning the rear windows with his goggles for any signs of detection from the property. None appeared, so he moved silently to the back of the house.

Removing his goggles and peering into the windows, his view was obscured by some old window netting. However, he could still make out 2 separate rooms. One was a disused room with some junk piled high. The second was the kitchen. There was a high ceiling and a stone floor. He saw some heavy cast iron pans hanging from a ceiling beam and a knife block reasonably close to the rear entrance. Useful in an ongoing fist fight, he thought. Looking through a small gap in one of the small square windows at the rear entrance, he saw a hall that led all the way down to the two rooms at the front of the building. To his left at the front of the house, a staircase climbed up to the top level, where he assumed they would find the Khalet's bedroom. The building was old and had not been maintained properly, so the rear door wasn't double glazed and it had an old Yale type lock. Aziz praised Allah, as this meant gaining entrance to the house would be relatively easy. If it was a double glazed door lock, he ran the risk of a key being stuck in the lock from the other side. Pretty impossible to pick in that situation, he thought.

Glancing upwards, he noticed the curtain twitch somewhat and assumed that an agent was watching the rear of the house from the back right hand side bedroom. Hiding in the garden shrubbery to his right, he waited for an hour and a half before he could hear the agents chatting at the next changing of the guard. Seizing the opportunity to make a retreat, he stuck to the borders of the garden, and moved quickly and silently to the rear of the property and over the wall.

Happy with his reconnaissance, Aziz made his way back to the nest, to await confirmation of the other routines they had previously observed, overnight.

When Abrafo woke later that morning, Aziz confirmed the routines and relayed his new data from the rear of the house. They retired to the van to discuss their strategy.

"Well Abrafo, we have two options, as far as I can see. We can raid them during the night when two of the agents are asleep. Entry to the house will be risky. We have no idea where the agents are and we run the risk of waking the other two. Depending on their level of experience and response time, we will have a struggle on our hands. This option is the riskiest because there are too many unknowns."

"Our second option, is to wait for the agent to get the coffee and disable him by the van. The time of day is in our favour, as two of the agents should still be asleep. You will exchange clothes with the coffee man and return with the coffee. I will gain entrance to the rear of the house and neutralise the agent who answers the door. Whilst you quickly deal with the two agents sleeping in the room to your right, I will subdue Mckenzie in the room on your left. Although this is still risky, I believe this is our best option. It is better to deal with the agents separately than to risk taking them all on together. Are we in agreement?"

Abrafo could see no other option based on the intelligence they had, so he agreed.

"So, how do we disable the coffee guy?" Said, The Mongoose.

Abrafo thought hard as he assessed the coffee shop and the car park in front of him through the windscreen. The van was parked in the south west corner of the car park and to the East, the coffee shop was directly in front of them. Beyond there, stood a small supermarket and another car park in between the two buildings. This would be difficult, he thought.

As the agent left the coffee store, they would have to manoeuvre the van in between the coffee shop and the agent, at just the right time to block his path, as well as the view from the supermarket. A rapid choke hold and he could be neutralised in the back of the van. A quick change into his clothes and they were on their way.

Aziz agreed it was the best plan, although there was a lot of risk. Especially considering they had only staked out the house for a few days, but Amir could not wait for a more thorough investigation, and as his father would say, "The winds do not blow as the vessels wish."

So, it was decided that Aziz would gain entry from the rear and Abrafo would be the distraction at the front, holding the coffee and a silenced pistol. It was the right decision, as Abrafo was a closer match in size to the coffee guy. Aziz prayed to Allah that the clothes were a good fit. Abrafo snatched what sleep he could in the back of the van and they waited until the trap could be sprung.

Chapter 29

The phone rang and startled Rathbone out of his daydream. He had been addressing The House on the implementation of the new Act and reassuring the public, and his corporate friends in the military industrial complex, that all the new security measures would be completed within the next five fiscal years. This would mean record profits year on year for him and his corporate friends. Not only did he have major investments in the companies that would provide the work, but they had given him substantial back handers through a secret Cayman Islands bank account, to ensure that the bountiful government contracts were assigned to them. It was a win win!

"Rathbone...Yes.... Yes. It's a great article, Nathan! Your father and I are so proud of the man you've become."

Rathbone opened the paper again to the centre spread on McKenzie. He smirked as he looked once again at the beautiful white church in the background of the garden picture.

"You have captured the spirit of this great country through your brilliant work at the paper, my boy. Getting him to endorse The Defence Act was a master stroke!"

Nathan had not printed what James had said about the act, at all. He had fabricated a jingoistic diatribe, about how James thought it was essential for the country to secure itself from outside invaders and terrorism, by fully embracing the Act.

"Yes…yes.. OK that would be fantastic. I'll arrange with your father and I look forward to seeing you there." Rathbone terminated the call.

Well that's our alibi complete, he thought. As long as the rag heads are successful and the Israeli doesn't find them in the meantime, we should have the perfect martyr for our cause! He subdued the thought of toasting his brilliance until after the event. He didn't want to jinx it. Everything hinged on the outrage and nationalistic fervour that could be created by the media's righteous crusade against the enemies of freedom and democracy, following the sad demise of our hero. Nathan had done a brilliant job, up to now. He just needed to play his part one more time.

Sir George couldn't have been happier with how things were unfolding. The more this Mckenzie chap was a national hero, the more his death would galvanise the vote.

Chapter 30

James was furious.

"...and here... halfway down the third paragraph, it quotes me as saying, 'I'm a staunch supporter of the Sovereign Territories Defence Act. The way these foreign terrorist cells are gaining entry to our beloved country and are able to operate with complete impunity, boils my blood.' I NEVER BLADDY SAID THAT!"

Alice held the phone away from her ear. They barely had 5 minutes to chat. She had been given an encrypted mobile by 'Tom', the guard's team leader... That was if Tom was even his name. She was weary and tired of this situation now, and just wanted to go back to normal life.

"I know James, they're a bunch of bastards! We knew this from the first interview! Look... let's take the money and run, yeah? Fuck them and their petty politics. I just want to take you and Andy, and run away now. Lets go somewhere hot and anonymous. I want to live the rest of our lives in peace and on permanent vacation."

Although they were so far apart, Alice and James felt close and affectionate for the first time since they could remember. That warmed James' soul and made him all the more keen to get back to his family. In spite of this, he still couldn't believe the cheek of that shit rag newspaper!

James had always hated the way the media outlets worked around the world. He knew they were experts in twisting the truth and emphasising only the parts of a story that suited their narrative. He had witnessed many moral crimes committed by the press in his lifetime, including phone tapping scandals, the horrendous lies printed about Hillsborough and the lies told about the miners strike, amongst other things. It was why he never bought newspapers anymore. They steered people away from the real, common issues that affect them all, and instead, have them arguing and bickering between themselves, over ridiculous subjects that keep them divided and docile. He firmly believed the media was a propaganda tool, used by the ruling class, to maintain their domain over society. This travesty just affirmed it to him. Alice had heard it all before though, so he let it go. They would take the newspapers money and run.

"Aye Petal. I miss ya both so much, Hen. I canny wait for this to be over and we can see each other again. Remember that day in June? Five years back? Andy won that football tournament and we had that picnic in the park. You looked so beautiful and I loved you so much, I thought my heart would burst. You have always been my girl, from the moment we met. I adore you my beautiful wife. Let's have another picnic, hey? "

Fresh, hot tears welled in Alice's eyes.

"James, I... I just want to say how fucking sorry I am, that I ever doubted you and the girl from work. I can't believe I was so stupid to believe the rumours over my own husband! I feel like a fool! That fucking dirty bastard next door had everyone's coat over their heads on this one, myself included! I just wanna tell you I love you so much and I'll never doubt you again." Alice burst into tears.

"Settle now, Hen." James said in a soothing voice," Its all come out in the wash now and he will get his, don't you worry. If I ever get my hands on that bastard, he will never have sex again! I promise you that, my love!"

They both laughed together for the first time in what seemed like eons.

"Right my Angel, give Andy a big kiss from me and tell him I'm proud of him and I'll call ye both tomorrow, if we are allowed. I gotta go. I'm getting the stink eye from my guy here haha. I love you so much and this will all be over soon, petal. I promise."

"Bye, my love." said Alice and hung up the phone.

It was 5.50pm and the spring light was fading. James liked this little Welsh village but he was keen to get back to normality, whatever that would be in the future, considering the money they had made and the unwanted fame. He was daydreaming of sunnier climes when there was a knock at the door. Ahh! the familiar sound of coffee arriving! Thought James, as he rubbed his hands together and smiled. He loved a proper coffee!

Sitting in the living room to the left of the entrance to the house, James heard a strange metallic click as the front door was opened, and the unmistakable sound of someone falling over. He got up to open the door, just as it was kicked open from the other side and to his horror, he saw the man who shot him on the motorway looming out of the hallway towards him. He let out a cry of shock and instinctively threw a right hook, but Aziz saw the attack coming and lithely dodged his fist, bringing his right hand up to James' chest as he pulled the trigger.

The last scene James witnessed as he was pulled into the hallway, was a dead agent on the stone floor and another man, emerging from the other agent's bedroom with a smoking gun.

Chapter 31

Horowitz was informed of Mckenzie's disappearance at 6.50 pm. The agents at the safe house had not responded to their half hourly check in with Vauxhall Cross at 6pm. A team was dispatched and arrived at 6.20pm. A brief check of the house and grounds for Mckenzie was futile, and they called it in at 6.45pm. Horowitz was uncharacteristically feeling the pressure. His bruised ego was seething with the audacity of these vermin.

"I DO NOT BELIEVE YOU!!" He barked at Amir.

"Please!! I beg you! I am telling the truth! Stop hurting my mother!" Begged Amir.

Jamila was trussed up against a large wheel type structure, her legs and arms splayed and she was naked, once again. One of the faceless was whipping her systematically with the 'Cat o' Nine Tails'. Deep black and purple bruises interspersed with older yellow marks created a stark contrast, where the fresh trauma had landed against her fragile skin. Bright red slivers seared the painful welts that littered her back. All the while, she screamed with all her might as each new impact landed.

"WHO ARE YOUR CONTACTS IN WALES!" Horowitz continued.

"We have no contacts in Wales or anywhere else, now!! They will all have disappeared after your raid. My brother will assume that I have collaborated and resorted to going dark. I will give you all the information I have please, please just stop!!"

Horowitz raised his hand and the flogging stopped. Amir was broken. The relentless beatings and sleep deprivation had taken its toll. Each time he would pass out from exhaustion, they would come screaming through the door with telescopic batons and pound him as a punishment. His face was swollen and contorted and his left eye completely closed over. He looked like a battered caricature of himself. Most of his teeth were missing, as they had been smashed out with a Hammer days ago, when he still had some fight left in him. The pain he felt was excruciating and he would tell them anything at all, just to save his mother, get some relief and to finally sleep.

"Bring the map," said Horowitz. A tablet device with a map of North Wales was passed over to him by one of his cohorts.

"We will get to the names of your disappearing contacts later, Amir. Now, I want you to put yourself in your brother's place. Tell me… Where would you take your captive in this area?"

Amir reasoned that his brother would not stay on the road in a vehicle, as he ran the risk of being detected by ANPR or CCTV at fuel stations and intersections. Each exposure to this network was added risk to his mission. He wouldn't chance it. Which left one alternative.

"Now that all of his options for a safe house are gone, my brother would still not risk retreating to hotels or motels for fear of being detected on camera. He will most likely look for a deserted farm building or out house within the area. The more secluded the better and yet it must have multiple options for escape. He would not risk travelling for more than 30 minutes as he would not be aware of your response time and would assume it was excellent. He would be cautious not to be mobile during any subsequent traffic search."

"OK. I want a list of all farms within a 30 minute radius of the safe house and I want them marked on the map." Snapped Horowitz," Time is of the essence, Gentlemen! Let's get to it!"

"Well done, Amir. You have shown you are willing to cooperate and as such, you have saved your mother from anymore unnecessary pain."

Whilst he was talking, two of the faceless released Jamila's broken body from the wheel and threw a gown at her. She slowly covered herself up wincing with the pain. She was taken away as Horowitz turned towards him again. His bespectacled beady blue eyes fixed on Amir. There was a flash of the wolf's teeth, as the cold stare of a predator in full control, pierced through Amir.

"... and now for the names and last known whereabouts of all your associates, Amir. Do not lie to me, as I will know."

Chapter 31

Horowitz was informed of Mckenzie's disappearance at 6.50 pm. The agents at the safe house had not responded to their half hourly check in with Vauxhall Cross at 6pm. A team was dispatched and arrived at 6.20pm. A brief check of the house and grounds for Mckenzie was futile, and they called it in at 6.45pm. Horowitz was uncharacteristically feeling the pressure. His bruised ego was seething with the audacity of these vermin.

"I DO NOT BELIEVE YOU!!" He barked at Amir.

"Please!! I beg you! I am telling the truth! Stop hurting my mother!" Begged Amir.

Jamila was trussed up against a large wheel type structure, her legs and arms splayed and she was naked, once again. One of the faceless was whipping her systematically with the 'Cat o' Nine Tails'. Deep black and purple bruises interspersed with older yellow marks created a stark contrast, where the fresh trauma had landed against her fragile skin. Bright red slivers seared the painful welts that littered her back. All the while, she screamed with all her might as each new impact landed.

"WHO ARE YOUR CONTACTS IN WALES!" Horowitz continued.

"We have no contacts in Wales or anywhere else, now!! They will all have disappeared after your raid. My brother will assume that I have collaborated and resorted to going dark. I will give you all the information I have please, please just stop!!"

Horowitz raised his hand and the flogging stopped. Amir was broken. The relentless beatings and sleep deprivation had taken its toll. Each time he would pass out from exhaustion, they would come screaming through the door with telescopic batons and pound him as a punishment. His face was swollen and contorted and his left eye completely closed over. He looked like a battered caricature of himself. Most of his teeth were missing, as they had been smashed out with a Hammer days ago, when he still had some fight left in him. The pain he felt was excruciating and he would tell them anything at all, just to save his mother, get some relief and to finally sleep.

"Bring the map," said Horowitz. A tablet device with a map of North Wales was passed over to him by one of his cohorts.

"We will get to the names of your disappearing contacts later, Amir. Now, I want you to put yourself in your brother's place. Tell me... Where would you take your captive in this area?"

Amir reasoned that his brother would not stay on the road in a vehicle, as he ran the risk of being detected by ANPR or CCTV at fuel stations and intersections. Each exposure to this network was added risk to his mission. He wouldn't chance it. Which left one alternative.

"Now that all of his options for a safe house are gone, my brother would still not risk retreating to hotels or motels for fear of being detected on camera. He will most likely look for a deserted farm building or out house within the area. The more secluded the better and yet it must have multiple options for escape. He would not risk travelling for more than 30 minutes as he would not be aware of your response time and would assume it was excellent. He would be cautious not to be mobile during any subsequent traffic search."

"OK. I want a list of all farms within a 30 minute radius of the safe house and I want them marked on the map." Snapped Horowitz," Time is of the essence, Gentlemen! Let's get to it!"

"Well done, Amir. You have shown you are willing to cooperate and as such, you have saved your mother from anymore unnecessary pain."

Whilst he was talking, two of the faceless released Jamila's broken body from the wheel and threw a gown at her. She slowly covered herself up wincing with the pain. She was taken away as Horowitz turned towards him again. His bespectacled beady blue eyes fixed on Amir. There was a flash of the wolf's teeth, as the cold stare of a predator in full control, pierced through Amir.

"... and now for the names and last known whereabouts of all your associates, Amir. Do not lie to me, as I will know."

Chapter 32

Not more than an hour after James' abduction, the mainstream media was all over the story. Broadcasts had been interrupted with the grave news of James disappearance and probable abduction by foreign insurgents on our sovereign soil. Twenty four hour news channels had live on the scene reporting and studio experts debated furiously, within a small set of parameters, as to who was to blame and what should be done about it.

Not one so called expert would challenge the real issues that caused this emergency. The endless wars for money. The subjugation of the "enemy" civilian population and the inevitable war crimes that followed, including murder, rape, torture and detainment without trial. The whitewashing of these crimes, by using terminology like "regime change" that was "necessary", in "politically unstable" "feral states". Repeating the lie over and over again, that these invasions are righteous, because they were bringing freedom and democracy to an oppressed nation. All the while, greedy western corporations would win contracts to rebuild the devastating damage caused by the war, to the infrastructure. The newly installed puppet government would line their own pockets and consolidate their power, by granting extortionate deals with the western corporations in order for them to fleece the valuable resources of that country, for a fraction of their worth.

Not one "expert", would show how these actions would always and without exception, breed motivated vengeful individuals, fuelled on catastrophic trauma and an insatiable desire to avenge their loved one's death. Every mother, father, daughter and son that was murdered in the name of "Democracy" and "Freedom", rest in silent witness to the obscene business of war. Their kin, left to rage and toil against those who they deem responsible, through brutal acts of terror and violence as the obscene cycle continues forever.

Instead, the mood was heavy on Nationalism, and "our patriotic duty to secure our island from these animals". The Sovereign Territories Defence Act was high on the agenda and all were in agreement, it was the right solution in such trying times.

There was hot debate on how the terrorists had found out about the location of the safe house and the story in The Daily National was brought to the fore. It was suggested that because Nathan Cromwell, Chief Editor, was the only person to visit him, and to publish the story and pictures of his reclusion; it was his negligence that led to the breach in security.

The most damning evidence of all, was a photograph taken in the garden of the safehouse. The grey white steeple of St Margaret's Church in Bodelwyddan was obviously how the terrorists got to him. There's only one church in Britain with John Gibson's tell tale limestone steeple! Obviously the terrorists had researched this, and from the information on the Internet, had worked out which building was the safe house.

Nathan sat silently seething opposite his father and Sir George Rathbone, who were sat at the exclusive table in the secret Gentlemen's Club in Mayfair. He had been duped and he didn't like it one bit. He would be expected to "take one for the team", which was OK for them! It wasn't their reputation on the line!

165

"Come now Nathan," Sir George waxed with a warm smile," your reputation will be restored in a few years. The public have a tendency to forget about these indiscretions. Especially when we feed them other distractions to get offended by. It will all blow over in a couple of years and your career will be back on track, my boy. More importantly, Nathan…. your future is secure! The contracts that your father's company will win, after the Act is passed in Parliament, means you stand to inherit millions. We can all get rich off the taxpayer, and all for the small price of one insignificant man's sacrifice." Sir George grinned at his father, who nodded in agreement.

Nathan stared at his father with a bemused look on his face. His father shrugged.

"I just don't like being hoodwinked in this way. You could have let me in on the plan. I look like an idiot!"

"Son, the less you know, the better for us all. Its called "Culpable Deniability". There are plans a foot that are far greater than you or I, but we can still profit from them, if we play the game correctly. If you want the finer things in life, sometimes you have to make sacrifices... now cheer up and eat your caviar."

Nathan snorted through his nose and sneered at them both.

"You better take care of me during and after this whole debacle. I want my career back and I want it more healthy than ever. "

"Don't worry Nathan, your sacrifice will not be forgotten." Sir George declared.

Later that evening, over the ring of Crystal Brandy glasses and with Cigars in hand, the three "Captains of Industry" toasted each other's success in the coming months and years.

The Distance Between Us

Chapter 33

Aziz was struggling to keep his anger in check, as Abrafo oriented the van through the narrow and overgrown B roads, within the Denbighshire borderlands. He was seething with anger. All of their current troubles were caused by this Khalet on the floor, hooded and bound in front of him. Back at the safe house, the taser had rendered James immobile, just long enough for the gag and hood to be placed on his head. His hands and feet were quickly tied, whilst Abrafo fetched the van and brought it from the 7-11 car park.

They had bundled him into the van with little care for staying incognito anymore. They had covered the registration plate with masking tape, anyway, so they had no fear of recognition in the immediate aftermath. They were so pumped, if anyone had tried to intervene, there would have been more bloodshed without a doubt. As it happened they sped away without incident and took to the hills to the south east.

Now a dark storm raged behind Aziz' eyes. He was torturing James by hitting him with a second bolt from the tazer, as soon as he had recovered from the last. He expected him to pass out, but this asshole was tough!

"allaenat ealayk 'ayuha alqadhir!!" Screamed Aziz," My brother better be OK and returned to me quickly, otherwise you will die a very slow painful death! you Son of a Dog!"

Aziz had a sadistic grimace across his face as he kept belting James. He took a perverse pleasure in watching James wince in pain with each new attack. Abrafo was starting to get nervous.

"My brother, stop now! If you continue, he will die and we will never see Amir again!"

Panting heavily with spittle hanging from his bottom lip, Aziz turned to glare at Abrafo in the driving seat. After a few seconds, he seemed to relent.

"You are right, my brother. I forget myself. Hurry on. We need to get settled and make contact for my brothers safe return."

There was no windows in the back of the van, so James had no idea where he was going. He tried to remember the turns and sounds from outside, but every time he was shocked, all he could concentrate on was the pain. He was not afraid. He was very angry. He knew not to let it out, but to control it. Like he was taught in boxing so many years ago, to control your anger is to have a valuable weapon when the time is right. He was already looking for opportunities to attack them and escape.

Although Aziz couldn't shock James anymore for fear of killing him, he was happy to punch and kick him with vengeful force. After what seemed like hours of intermittent pain to James, the van slowed to a crawl, as the sun was fading through the windscreen.

Wherever they were taking him, they had arrived. James was immediately dragged from the van and dropped on the hard stone floor outside. He was punched a few times more and dragged from the van across a small yard, and into what he believed to be a derelict building. The smell of moss, lichen and damp walls hung in the air.

There was hardly any light inside, as there was only one small window and it didn't face the sunset. It was starting to get cold as the day waned. James shivered. He was thrown into the corner of the room, where some heavy rubble and shattered bricks broke his fall. He winced again as he hit the hard, jagged mound.

Aziz took out the next encrypted burner phone from his pocket, turned it on and called Albert Embankment.

" Good Evening, how may I direct your call?"

"Shut up and listen carefully. This is the Light of Mohammed. Today, we seized James McKenzie from your agents and we are making our demands known for his safe release."

 At MI6 headquarters, the receptionist signalled contact with the insurgents, by putting his thumb in the air and a flurry of activity engulfed the room. A trace was started and a team of agents began listening to the conversation.

"Whom is it I am speaking to, please?", said the receptionist, trying to slow down the conversation. He knew they needed as much time on the call as possible in order to triangulate the assailant's whereabouts.

"You already know my name. Our demands are as follows." Barked Aziz.

"Number one. We demand the release of my brother, Amir, taken from the roadside.

Number two. We demand the release of the Cleric Abu Hassan from HMP Wakefield and last,

We demand safe transportation for all of us to Oman, in a private jet plane.

We will guarantee the release of James McKenzie, when we land at Muscat International Airport and our onward journey is secure. These demands are not negotiable. Failure to deliver on any of them will result in Mckenzie's death. I will call again soon to confirm the details of our travel."

Foiling the attempt to trace the call, he abruptly hung up and smashed the phone to bits with a rock. Now we wait, he thought.

Looking at Abrafo, he said, "Bring in the blankets and some food. There will be no fires until this is over."

James shivered again. Looks like I'm in for a cold night, he thought to himself. Abrafo returned around fifteen minutes later. He had stealthily moved the van behind the abandoned cottage they had chosen and tried to camouflage it with some broken branches that littered the floor. He had some tinned food and a few blankets.

James got none of it.

The Arabs wrapped themselves in the blankets, whilst Abrafo stood guard at the window with his Argentine rifle. Aziz ate whatever was in the tin, cold with a spoon. James heard the clank, but could not see what is was because he was still hooded.

Aziz continued to seethe. The last three weeks had been one disaster after another. He had been living on his wits and the stress had almost shot his judgement to bits. He blamed James entirely, for his predicament. If he hadn't have gotten out of his car and hit his brother, they would all be safe. Why didn't he just stay on the ground? Why did he have to be the fucking hero?!

These questions ate away at Aziz as he sat there scowling at James with each mouthful, until he just had to ask him. He stood up and aggressively removed the hood and the tape that was gagging James. James cried out, as the tape ripped the last few days stubble growth from his cheeks. Aziz cupped James mouth and talked in his ear.

"DO NOT cry out or scream. No one will hear you anyway, and I will beat you and put the tape back on. Do you understand?"

James looked him dead in the eye and nodded with a small grimace on his face.

"Good.

You are the reason why we are here McKenzie… You are the reason why my brother is probably being tortured and beaten for information…. When I look at your pale disgusting face, all I see is why I detest your way of life so much.

You and your countrymen are oblivious to the harm your government does to our brothers and sisters in our homelands. You languish on your sofas every night, watching trash television and social media that is, by design, made to keep you looking inwards at yourselves and not asking questions about these obscene acts, carried out by every successive Christian onslaught for the last two thousand years!

You sit believing all you hear on your news channels. The programming, so subtle, the audience don't even know they are being brainwashed! Lies and distraction fed to your people, like some universal anaesthetic, keeping you all asleep, whilst you gorge yourselves on alcohol and drugs, in a futile attempt to forget that you are all wage slaves to your masters!

So called "reality" TV shows that make you feel that you can aspire to great things. 'You too could be a millionaire if you just work hard enough!' Right? Ha! 'Look at these rich women fight over petty ridiculous things, whilst they wallow in their ostentatious, obscene wealth!' You want to know what "reality" is McKenzie?!

Reality, is the murder of loved ones, the destruction of homes, the terror and torture of family members, detainment without charge, abduction and rape, the stealing of resources and the collapse of civilisation in every country that your government have invaded, on the back of outright lies!"

"All the while Mckenzie, you and your kind lap it up, like you're the stars of your own TV shows. Regurgitating what you've seen and heard from the propaganda on your social media and televisions, declaring these ideas as your own, when really, you don't have a fucking clue you've been programmed! Your kind continuously follow the narrative, spoon fed to them by your government, through official news stations and current affairs talk shows! You make me sick!"

Aziz was red in the face, spitting and gesticulating wildly. He was ranting and had adopted a mocking tone.

"I ask you this, Mckenzie.... Did you jump from your car knowing you would be on everyone's Television? Did you believe this was your chance at fame? Did you think your actions would make you a famous hero?"

Aziz sprang toward James and gripped him with both hands by his collar.

"Why did you get involved? Why did you hit my brother? Answer me!!"

James sat shaking his head. He thought before he answered. He felt no anger towards this man, only empathy and understanding to what he was intimating. James chose his words carefully.

"You and I... We are so different in so many ways. I don't know what it takes to drive a man to mass murder hundreds of strangers in a foreign land. Maybe you're closer to the psychopaths and sociopaths that are rewarded by this flawed system in which we are all forced to live.

Believe me when I say this; I sympathise with the families who have lost loved ones to terrorism from all sides, including my own government. So I say that we are similar in some ways, too.

You believe that we sit back and are complicit with the wrongs our government does and yet you don't know the half of it. You are right when you say that our society is being programmed to focus on unachievable goals. Celebrity culture is a distraction that makes people believe that dreams do come true. The general public around the world, not just in the west, have all bought into this idea as an escape from the monotonous prison that our social system has become.

Yes! they believe the lie that hard work can lift them out of their slavery because they want so badly to believe it! ...and yet... I know, like you, that the system is rigged in favour of those with the most money.

So, in answer to your question. No... I didn't help those people for fame or fortune. I did it because those people were going to die. There was no one else there to save them and I would want someone to do it for me, or the people I loved, if they were in the same situation!

I wasn't attacking you or your brother. I was trying to help you! Your brother punched me and then you shot me! ... and yet I'm the bad guy?! You're fucking dreaming, lad!"

James was getting irate.

"Look, you want to know how I see the world? Millennia ago, some idiots decided it would be a good idea to exchange tokens for resources and money was invented. Sure enough it served society well, in some ways, but what they didn't account for was greed.

Skip a 1000 years down the line and now those people and families who have benefitted from the slow accumulation of this wealth, can now buy anyone and anything! All because our social system continues to use money as a tool to exchange resources.

If you have enough money in today's society, you can even buy the very thoughts in people's heads!

You can literally buy the minds of the general public and tell them what to believe! It's all done through advertising, social media and the news.

Our government is chosen by the Corporations, through the power of the media. Television has the magical ability to change public opinion. All because of a innocent flaw in the human condition. The fact that, people will believe anything you tell them, if you say it for long enough. The people with the real power know this and they are the ones with the most money.

The politicians, who make huge sums of money assisting the agendas of the corporations, then make the laws that ensure the wealth remains in the hands of the few and therefore so does the power.

You believe God's name to be Allah but I know God's name to be Money."

Aziz was a little taken aback. He had not expected this tirade. Inwardly he was a little impressed by James' fervour and more to the point, he had made an interesting observation that Aziz hadn't before... Real power comes from the control of resources that can only be exchanged for money! It was never about religion! It was so obvious, now he said it. Aziz was more than a little disappointed in himself.

"Money.... Yes.... It is ALL about making money, isn't it? Each one of those bombs that is dropped must be paid for... And who pays? The tax payer, of course... so the costs are inflated, the shareholders get huge dividends and the media spin the patriot story, just enough to keep the public buying into the idea of the common enemy..."

"Yes!!" Exclaimed James," but don't you see? You come along and set the world on fire and all your doing is stoking the bullshit and reaffirming the need for these wars in the first place!

It's a vicious cycle based on generating wealth for the chosen few!! You're not changing the world with these terrorists attacks, you are helping them to maintain it!"

Aziz sat back. He felt deflated and fought to deny the feelings of futility, breeding like mold in his mind. He could not escape the feeling that the actions of the Light of Mohammed were directly responsible for perpetuating this obscene market. He despaired when he realised that all that they had been fighting for, could be reduced to trading the lives and souls of his people and his victims, for numbers on a Wall Street screen.

Just then, James felt a blinding crack to his temple and a great flash of white light. He grunted and fell down to his left. The right side of his head felt like it was on fire.

"SHUT YOUR INFIDEL MOUTH, CHELB!!" Abrafo screamed. He had had enough of this bastards whiny words! How dare he dishonour Allah's name by comparing him to money! and then having the cheek to say that we are the terrorists! He had struck James hard with the butt of his rifle. The disturbance shook Aziz from his thoughts and it was enough to shift his concentration back to the mission.

James stayed silent on the floor for fear of another beating. Meanwhile, Abrafo returned to his post, snorting and grimacing like the Beast of the Earth, as it will emerge from the hills of Safa.

Chapter 34

The Israeli was deep in thought as the cavalcade swept west along the A55 and into North Wales. His team had worked methodically to prioritise locations by how isolated they were and the most time saving way they could clear each site. The first of which was just 5 mins away.

Horowitz would step back and let the tactical team take the lead when they reached the target area. He wouldn't get involved until the dirty work was done. The main priority was to capture the remaining terrorists. Solomon knew they had invaluable information and so it was imperative that they were taken alive. Taking Mckenzie alive was a secondary objective, but not necessary for the success of the mission.

"Two minutes!" barked the commander in the front of the SUV. The sound of a flurry of weapons and equipment checks filled the air and then there was an intense silence, a product of the focus and concentration etched on the operatives' faces as they pulled off the road.

The leading SUV pulled up as two of the faceless exited and launched a drone with a single throw. Horowitz had a feed from the drone as it prowled the night sky in search of their quarry.

"No vehicles detected. Switching to infrared."

The drone picked up no heat signatures outside the abandoned cottage, but there was two, maybe three possible signatures seen through the window of the first room.

"Teams. Move in to position."

Using their night vision headsets, the teams moved as one, encircling the building with precision and stealth. Team one approached the entrance. The soldier on point threw in a stun grenade and after a few seconds, they stormed in.

The vanguard, working on pure muscle memory and instinct, opened fire as a large white mass loomed out of the darkness.

The goat hit the floor, as it's counterparts screamed and leaped wildly in the background. The injured Goat cried and garbled in pain, as the blood rushed into its oesophagus from the open wound in its throat. One of the faceless quickly put it out of its misery.

"Building cleared! Search unsuccessful. Just some goats seeking shelter for the night." The commander of the team reported.

Horowitz shook his head. They were in for a long night.

"Onto the next target at the double!" He shouted as the teams reassembled and boarded the cavalcade.

Quickly, they sped on into the night.

Chapter 35

Aziz had been on the phone to MI6 again and they had employed the usual tactic of trying to stall him. He would call again in an hour and if he had no answers, he would have to resort to some dirty tricks to get them moving on their end. They must understand he meant business! Maybe he would send a video call of him amputating one of Mckenzie's hands…

It was Aziz' turn to stand on watch and he had left the building to walk the perimeter. He had been thinking a lot about what James had said and he was exploring the possibility that he had been fighting the wrong battle.

What if Mckenzie was right? What if the idea was to create an enemy, and then go to war just to sell massive amounts of arms for huge sums of money, just so the powerful could amass even more money and power?

Aziz was starting to feel duped. It wasn't at all about the Western Powers believing that his racial brothers were an evil Ideology. That was the fallacy the western media fed to their voters, in order to sell the idea of a war!

Well if this was true, then the average western person is still culpable! He thought. They are guilty of the crimes as well as their leaders, simply because they do NOTHING to prevent their governments and corporations from committing these crimes in the first place! In their so called democracy, they have the power to vote war mongers out of office and yet, they choose to believe their lies instead. He remained as resolute as ever in his commitment to his cause. These infidels have lost their way and renounced the will of his God. It was his duty to Allah to scourge them from the Earth. He continued on his patrol.

Back in the hovel, James was staring intently at Abrafo. They had left him without his hood and had not put the tape back on his mouth, because James had complained that he couldn't breathe properly through his nose. In reality, James wanted at least half a chance to change their perspective on who the real enemy is. Abrafo wasn't concerned, anyway. After smashing James with his rifle, he thought that would be enough of a deterrent against him talking... and yet, he would not stop staring at him.

"What the fuck are you looking at?" Sneered Abrafo. James shrugged with a look of disdain and said nothing.

"You think you're better than me, don't you?" Abrafo jibed.

"Not at all," said James," I'm different to you, that's for sure, but no better off in the great scheme of things...I do think you're fucking stupid, though."

Abrafo bridled at that.

"Why am I the stupid one, Nadhl? You are the one in chains!" He scoffed.

"You just don't get it, do you Pal? I'm not your enemy. Although we are miles apart in our culture and in a lot of our beliefs... We have more in common than you realise."

Abrafo shook his head.

"It was white men like you, that led the gangs that murdered their way across my country. One of these gangs raped and killed my mother in front of me, just so men like you could buy the diamonds, stolen from our children's hands, to put on the hands of your fat, bloated, lazy and complicit women. We have nothing in common."

James shook his head.

"Look, Pal. I'm sorry about your mother. That's a horrific thing to happen to anyone. That being said, I am not complicit in that crime just because I am white.

This is why our species is doomed. You look to see the differences between us, rather than what we have in common and it's not your fault. It's a tactic to keep us under control."

"No one controls me!" declared Abrafo.

James thought how he could explain what he meant.

"Look…It's like this… If you were born into fortunes of money or acquired it through lucky commercial means, you would quickly realise the power and influence you gain from monetary wealth. Suddenly, people will be more pleasant to you. You can get people to do the shitty things you don't want to do for yourself, by giving them money. Everyone wants to do things for you because you will give them money to do it."

"Of course," said Abrafo in a dismissive way. This man thinks I am an idiot! He thought.

"...But listen, Pal. It's not the money they love, or you for that matter. It's the access to the resources that they need, which they can only access, by exchanging the money that they receive, for selling some of their limited time before they die. This is the flaw in our society. Those with wealth can enslave those without wealth into doing those tasks for them, otherwise, those without wealth cannot access the resources that they need to live."

Abrafo snorted through his nostrils.

"How are people enslaved? You do a job, you get paid! Simple!" He said.

"Look, Pal..." said James. "Money is just a token you exchange for your time. The true value of your time as a worker, is not given back to you as money, though. Your employer steals a little of the true value of your labour and calls it profit.

The concept of profit is how we are enslaved."

"Over time, that profit that was stolen, travels higher up the monetary economic pyramid until it becomes a vast wealth of "time" in the upper echelons. Now, those with the vast wealth don't have to swap their own "time" to access resources, they can use the profit, or time, stolen from their workers!"

Abrafo remembered his mother's protest at the mine, and how it was because the workers were paid in pennies and they were forced to work in terrible conditions. Some of those workers were doing twelve hour shifts, seven days a week and barely getting enough money to pay rent and eat. They were slaves in everything but name. He let James continue.

"Now, if you had vast sums of wealth and free time, wouldn't you want to protect the system that rewarded you with the best of everything? Wouldn't you want to guarantee your precious children's access to those resources in the future, maybe even to the detriment of other people's children?

Don't get me wrong, I'm not excusing this behaviour in any way. I just want you to understand that the monetary economic system of resource distribution, at it's foundation, is fundamentally flawed. Having a "free market" where profits are not capped, results in a system that is easily exploited by the greedy and the selfish.

This system at it core, promotes the exploitation of those people on the lower levels of the economic pyramid. The exploitation that occurs with every transaction, at each level of the pyramid, understandably rewards those without any conscience. This system actively promotes psychopathic and sociopathic behaviour, and as such, over hundreds of years, it has put those very same psychopaths in the seats of power, that rule and govern the nations of the world.

Men and women without empathy, who are driven by ego and an inflated sense of self worth. They have the power to end universal suffering across the planet, but instead choose to perpetuate this flawed system, through a media web of lies and deceit, because it feeds their insatiable lust for power and domain over their brothers and sisters from across the globe. Those very same brothers and sisters that, by birthright of being born on this planet, should have access to all the resources of it and yet, they are being withheld from them, unless they have the right amount of imaginary credits, which they can only attain through profiting off their fellow human beings!"

"This is the Capitalist dream of success and I tell ya this, if you or I were given the opportunity, we would behave in exactly the same way because we have been indoctrinated into thinking there is no alternative.

However, my friend, there is an alternative."

Abrafo didn't have the capacity to see the big picture and it was starting to confuse him. He thought that James was saying that he was either a Psychopath or a Slave.

"You talk nonsense, Mckenzie! I have worked my way from the gutter to be the man I am today. I have vast amounts of wealth in offshore accounts because of MY hard work! I am no slave!... You may think I am a Psychopath but you are wrong! I am a hero to my people! A freedom fighter against the evil infidels that steal our children's futures!"

"Yes! I'm sure you are! Yet, wouldn't it be better if you didn't have to fight at all? What would you do if you didn't have to fight?" said James.

Abrafo was caught off guard by the question. He had often dreamed of another life. A peaceful life. One with a family and a wife. He dreamed of owning his own farm back home and growing fruit.

"I would be a farmer." He said, in a far away tone.

James nodded and continued.

"Ok, well imagine a world where resources are not distributed by money, but by need and desire! Imagine a world where robots do the hard work and create an abundance of resources in a way that protects the planet instead of destroying it with mindless consumerism! Imagine that every crumb of food and every drop of water was not wasted and given to people regardless of their ability to buy it! This would free us all to pursue the things we love to do, in a world were politics, borders, poverty, war and crime don't exist!

This world is achievable if we swapped our Monetary Based Economy for a Resource Based Economy. As a society, we just need to stop using money to distribute resources!"

Abrafo thought James had lost his mind and looked on incredulously.

"I know you think I'm mad, but the greatest obstacle to this beautiful Utopia, is getting rid of "Money". This is because the Psychopaths and Sociopaths who own the vast amounts of wealth, will never relinquish the power it gives them."

"They are so short sighted, they cannot see that everyone, including themselves, can live in luxury far greater than they have right now, if only they embraced this new social system. So, in order to protect their way of life, they must hide behind smoke and mirrors. They must keep the masses attention away from the massive flaws and social problems that the current social system creates and direct it elsewhere…. and how do they do it?

By creating differences between us.

Politics, Religion, Wars, Social Culture, Gender, wage differences, sports teams, Celebrity Culture… All of these things, from the smallest jibe under your breath to the largest social persecutions, create a society of competition, division and discontent. In the worst cases, the wealthy create enemies for their slaves to hate and destroy. If they keep us fighting between ourselves, we won't be fighting for an alternative way of life, will we?"

"Think about it, advancements in communication technology and transportation should mean the world is more connected and yet the people have never been more divided. Those differences that have been indoctrinated into you and me since birth, through subtle prejudices and the bigotry that runs through the very fabric of our society, have created a massive distance between us all. A distance created in our minds. A distance that is perpetuated by these technologies, when they could be used to bring us together in collaboration, rather than dividing us through competition."

James looked down forlornly, shaking his head.

"Don't you see, Pal?...

...It's the distance between us, that keeps us enslaved."

Abrafo was not a critical thinker. He was confused and hungry and he was sick of listening to this idiot.

"Shut up, now! You are giving me a headache! May Allah strike you down if you keep up this nonsense!" He barked.

"For fucks sake, man! I'm trying to help you understand here!" James exclaimed.

James was getting pissed off now. These bastard people had stolen his life from him. James would never be able to go back to his normal life. Not only that, he had also tried his very best to show them that they were one and the same, but it was falling on deaf ears. All he wanted to do, was to go back to his plain old life with his beautiful wife and son. Oh, how he missed them!

"So what's your motive here, Pal?" said James in a curt tone.

" Do you think you're doing your God's work? Hmm? Do you believe in a God, do you?? An invisible man in the sky who watches your every move, yes?

How do you think he feels about you blowing innocent kids to pieces with those bombs of yours, hey? Do you think your god believes children are a legitimate target, now?"

"HOW DARE YOU?!" Screamed Abrafo," Your governments have always seen our children as legitimate targets!!"

James wasn't listening now. They had been over this.

"There are thousands of deities across the world that are being worshipped and you think yours is the one true god? EVERYONE believes their god is the one!" James shouted.

"If this God exists, why does he hide? Why not come out and say hello? Let us know he's the one true god? If he is omnipotent, why does he allow Satan to exist? Why does he allow the bad things to happen in the world? Like… like… Childhood cancer for one! What the fuck did those kids do to deserve that?!

The universe is infinite and you think a god created it? This God would have to be bigger than the universe… that is infinite!...you understand the physical problem with that, yes?" James was laughing hysterically now.

"Let me enlighten you, lad! … There is no fucking god! Your god allowed your mother to be raped and murdered in front of you and you still adore 'him'? Why did he let that happen to a sweet young lad like you? What the fuck did you do to deserved that, hey?

Like all major organised religions, they are a lie, created out of the socio economic problems that each part of the world faced at the time. They are fairy stories, lad. Designed to make you do the abhorrent things that men like you do, but conveniently without a conscience."

James was ranting.

"SHUT UP ABOUT MY MOTHER!! SHUT UP! SHUT UP!!"
Screamed Abrafo, but James was relentless.

"You think you will see your mother in paradise? She's gone, lad.
There is no paradise and you'll never see her again. She is dead
forever. Even if she was, she would probably disown you for your
sins and watch you burn in your hell!"

This was too much for Abrafo and he snapped. Like all bullies who
have no argument, he resorted to violence. He struck James hard,
over and over again with the butt of his rifle. Abrafo was raging.
Eyes bloodshot and wide from lack of sleep, a terrifying grimace
pierced the darkness as he grunted like a beast, with each massive
and brutal blow.

James head became a mash of blood and bone, his nose and jaw
broken and one of his eyes burst as Abrafo rained down his
vengeance.

In Abrafo's mind, he was reliving his mother's humiliation and
murder, feeling the impotence of that little boy again, who could do
nothing to save his 'Mama' from the monsters. These devastating
and traumatic memories, fuelled the adult rage that erupted in such
hatred and violence.

In James mind, through the pain and fear, all he could think about
was that beautiful day in the sun, watching his son play football
whilst his darling wife prepared the picnic. The sun, glistening
through her hair, as she smiled her beautiful smile and kissed him
with pure love on the lips, holding his face in her soft hands.

He had never felt so in love with his wife and his boy, and as he slipped away, he enveloped himself in that love, until eventually, he succumbed to the cold, comforting embrace of oblivion.

…

At that moment, Aziz burst into the hovel. He had heard the commotion from thirty feet away as Abrafo had raged. The sight that beheld him was truly grotesque and filled him with despair.

"Abrafo!!" He quietly exclaimed with utter tearful disbelief, "what.. have.. you DONE!!"

Aziz eyes, growing wider first in denial and then through livid understanding, turned on Abrafo, as an insurmountable, terrifying, anger filled his battle worn face.

"WHAT HAVE YOU DONE?! MY BROTHER IS GONE YOU FUCKING IDIOT! WE CAN NEVER GET HIM BACK NOW!!!"

Abrafo looked jaded as he gasped for breath. He knew he had made a terrible mistake and fell to his knees, hands clasped tight in submission.

"Ohhh! My brother! I'm so sorry! It happened so quickly! He was taunting my mother's death!" Abrafo tried to justify his actions once more, by deflecting to his God.

"Allah guided my hand!"

Aziz, looking down on the unrecognisable mess of James' head, realised all was lost. In a split second he accepted the terrible truth.

He would never see his brother again.

The grief and despair that enveloped him, took the strength from his legs and he stumbled where he stood. The Mongoose let out a long, low groan of despair as he looked down at James and tears welled in his eyes.

He changed his gaze to Abrafo who was now prostrate on the floor, as if praying to Mecca. Aziz raised his rifle and shot Abrafo in the back of the head. Blood and brains spattered the rocks beneath him, as Aziz cried out in rage and despair.

Within minutes, after gathering his thoughts and some essential supplies, Aziz slipped away into the uncertain night.

Chapter 36

A ndrew McKenzie stood outside the Army Recruitment Centre on Watergate Street in the city. He took the last drag on the reefer he'd made before jumping on the train that morning. All this will have to stop soon, he thought. The Army doesn't like druggies. He stumped it out and brushed himself off.

In the year since his father had been murdered, so much had happened, that Andy still felt like he had not had a chance to grieve for him. His dad had been practically raised as a martyr by the mainstream press, including the Daily National, who's new editor in chief had called on the King to posthumously award James the George Cross, for his 'Heroism and Gallantry in circumstances of extreme danger'. The Monarchy had fully agreed and James McKenzie was inducted into that small group of heroes, forever.

The Sovereign Territories Defence Act was passed unanimously, through both houses of Parliament.

Huge sums of public money and contracts were given to certain corporations in order to implement the infrastructure, that would enforce the new draconian laws written into the Act. To those in the know, this would be the greatest movement of wealth from the public purse into the hands of the few, that any British government had ever presided over.

This was "Mission Accomplished" for Rathbone, who recieved a hereditary peerage and "retired" to the House of Lords.

Andy's mum Alice, had gone off the rails and lost herself in the bottle. The money from the paper lay untouched in the bank, since James' death. Both Andy and Alice couldn't bear to touch it. They thought it was blood money from the Daily National. Money to buy their silence, about the paper being to blame for the lapse in security, that led to James' murder. Alice and Andy wanted to donate it to charity but hadn't decided on which one yet. They hadn't spoken for a while.

Andy had been looking after himself a lot lately, as his mum was often missing when he got home from school. Usually propping up the bar in town, sneering at anyone and everyone. He was convinced she spent so much time there because she couldn't face looking at Andy anymore, as he reminded her so much of his dad.

He'd sat his exams but he held no hope of a single pass. His head wasn't in it. All he could think about since his dad was killed, was joining up. He hadn't told his mother, she probably wouldn't be bothered anyway. He'd seen the Army Recruitment advert on the TV over, and over again about finding out "...where you belong." It suggested that he'd find a family when he joined up and he liked that idea. There was something romantic that appealed to lads of his age, about a bunch of misfits coming together and fighting for each other. If he was killed in combat, at least it would be an honourable death.

He breathed a heavy sigh and looked into the dark rain clouds above.

"This one's for you, Dad."

Then, Andrew McKenzie, 16 years old, opened the door to the Army Careers Office, and another catastrophically traumatised child was radicalised, by the relentless business of war. Not one passer-by noticed or cared, as the cold, grey rain, battered the weeds trying their best to survive, whilst they strained for a glimmer of light, pushing through the cracks in the stone pavement.

Printed in Great Britain
by Amazon

30119476R00109